Good Grief
A Journey of Healing

Myron Miller, MD, and Christie L. Ollar

Copyright © 2017 by Myron Miller, MD and Christie Ollar
All rights reserved. This book or any portion thereof may not be reproduced or used in any manner whatsoever without the express written permission of the author except for the use of brief quotations in a book review.

Scripture quotations taken from the Holy Bible, English Standard Version, Copyright © 2008. Used by permission of Crossway, a publishing ministry of Good News Publishers. All rights reserved. ESV text edition: 2011.

Editor: Rebekah Peiffer
Book layout by Heather Westbrook, www.hwdesigns.info
First Printing, 2017
Printed by CreateSpace, An Amazon.com Company
ISBN-13: 978-1978222007
ISBN-10: 1978222009

Photo Credits
Audra J. Gilbert: Scree, p.40; Uncertainties, p.46
Christie L. Ollar: New Terrain, p.16; Bushwhacking, p.22; Stuck, p.56; The Summit, p.60; Monuments, p.62
Faith Layton: Obstacles, p.50
Gary R. Funck: The Unchosen Path Poem, p.6; Introduction, p.12; Loss of Control, p.24; A Clearing, p.36; Unnecessary Burdens, p.44
Myron & Doreen Miller Family: The Trail Traveled, p.30; The View, p.52; Blisters, p.58; Trail's End (or not?), p.64
Natalie Snyder: The Reluctant Hike, p.14; Lost, p.18; Fatigue, p.32; Despair, p.34; Travel Companions, p.42; Muscle Cramps, p.54
Anita Atkins: Contents, p.8; Author Addendum, p.66; Vending Machine God Poem, p.68
Public domain photos from pexels.com: Cover; Fog, p.20; Vertigo, p.28; Don't Feed the Bears, p.48; Back Cover
Public domain photos from unsplash.com: Preface, p.10; Darkness, p.26; Storms, p.38

Dedications

Dedicated to Josh Ollar (10/23/77 - 9/12/14), my friend and brother-in-law, who is now exploring all of Heaven, climbing every mountain, and hiking every trail. One day we will join him there.
-Christie

Dedicated to my dad, Mahlon Miller (4/2/31 - 7/18/14), who started life as an Amish farm boy and went on to be a Mennonite pastor. He gave me a love for God's creation, a joy in reading books, and encouragement for pursuing my dreams.
-Myron

Endorsements

"I very much appreciated the text, not only for its wisdom but also for the experience of real grief that has made such reflections possible. This is . . . emerging from the questions and darkness that the insanity this broken world creates.

We don't get through life without an invitation to hike up Grief Mountain. Christie Ollar and Myron Miller have been up that mournful mountain . . . and have given the rest of us a trail map . . . and the encouragement to continue to hike even when it feels overwhelming, for there is grace along the way. Beyond the care and comfort provided by loved ones and the God who suffers with us is the companionship offered by the authors, who know of what they speak. Tap into their wisdom for your own inevitable, occasional journey through the dark night of grief."

- Dr. Tony Blair, Ph.D., D. Min. President, Evangelical Theological Seminary (Myerstown, PA)

"As a hospice nurse, I often find myself on the grief path. This beautifully written book . . . is a graceful illustration of the path of grief. Many lives will be forever touched by the words they have written."

- Andrea Gordner, RN, Hospice Nurse

"Reading *Good Grief* feels like sitting by a fireplace with an old friend, pondering some of life's toughest emotions. Myron and Christie have walked the mountain of grief in their own lives, and their musings gently encourage those trying to find their way through difficult times. This is not a formula for erasing hurt; rather, this book speaks truth to readers as they walk bravely along the path of loss. For those who don't know how to help a friend or loved one who is facing a loss, this book provides invaluable insight. Myron and Christie are the perfect traveling companions. Their candid and personal insights acknowledge that although the path may be long, comfort and peace can be found in the journey."

- Natalie A. Snyder, M.Ed., language educator

"*Good Grief* is a much-needed book on the topic of grief and will provide easy-to-grasp concepts for those needing time and safety to grieve well."

- David W. Musser, LMFT (licensed marriage and family therapist)

"We all face times when we go through the grieving process. For anyone taking that journey, Myron Miller and Christie Ollar have prepared a marvelous tool to aid in the healing process."

- Gary Messinger, Pastor

"The death of a loved one changes our lives forever. What can be expected? What is normal? Myron Miller and Christie Ollar help walk us through this difficult time.

I know the wisdom they share will resonate with you. The journey will still be difficult, but knowing others understand and have walked this trail as well will lighten the burden and give clarity to the emotions you are experiencing during your time of grief. As you read this book, you will feel their understanding heart and know that God cares and loves you deeply. That message alone is priceless."

- Stephen P. Lum, BMS (Bachelor of Mortuary Science), Licensed Funeral Director

"*Good Grief* is a wonderful guide on the difficult trek through dealing with the loss of a loved one. Having walked this path, . . . I am glad to have this resource. With its thoughtful analogies and helpful suggestions, it will be a useful source for my patients, my family, and myself as we face one of the most difficult trials of this life, the trail leading up Grief Mountain."

- M. Chad Banks, PA-C, MPAS (Masters in Physician Assistant Studies)

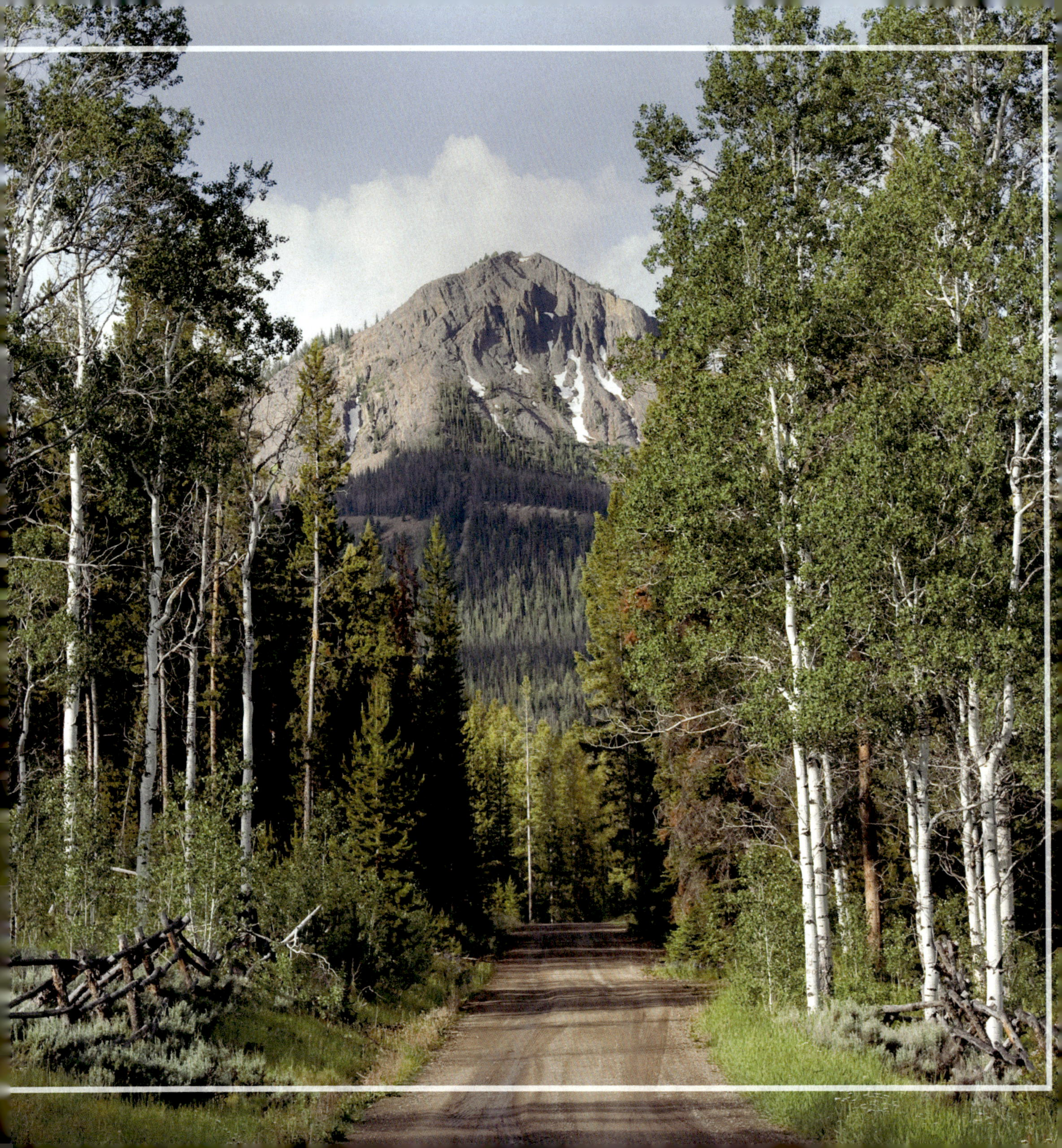

The Unchosen Path

By Christie Ollar

I didn't choose to walk this path;
no one ever would.
It seems unfair, an unkind fate,
I'd turn back if I could.

Yet here I stand and look around,
"Am I really here?"
Reality sets in my mind,
confirming all I fear.

As though dazed I take a step
on this long path of dirt.
It stretches past my blurry gaze
a hard terrain of hurt.

But where will this path take me?
What's the purpose, where's the end?
There's so much I don't understand,
my mind can't comprehend.

I'm forced to trust what I can't see,
and walk where I've not been.
To be guided and let grief evolve,
to a healing deep within.

And so I'll go, each step in faith,
and pray for strength each day.
As loss brings forth a new rebirth,
the path will guide my way.

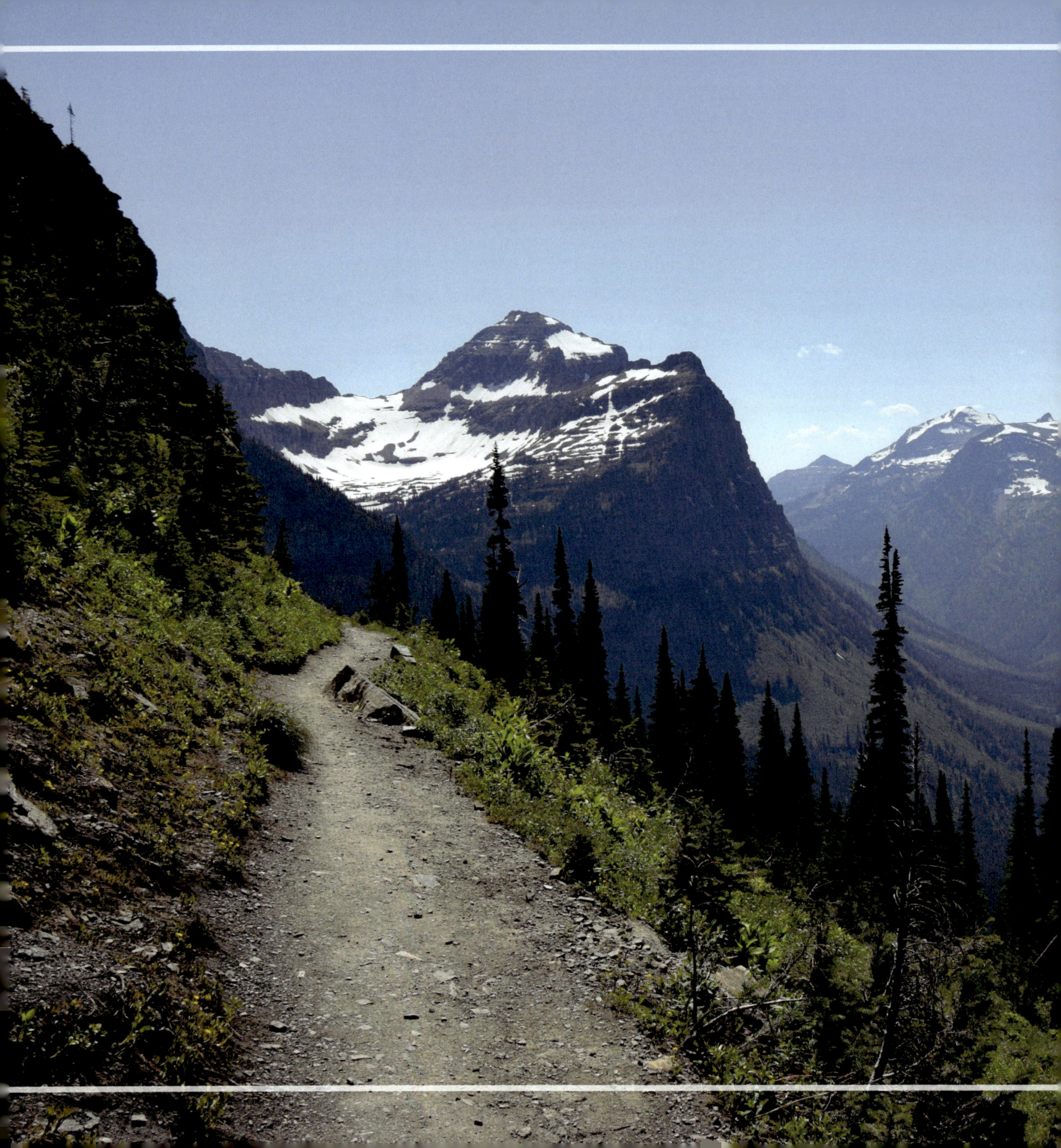

Contents

Preface	11
Introduction	12
The Reluctant Hiker	15
New Terrain	17
Lost	19
Fog	21
Bushwhacking	23
Loss of Control	25
Darkness	27
Vertigo	29
The Trail Traveled	31
Fatigue	33
Despair	35
A Clearing	37
Storms	39
Scree	41
Travel Companions	43
Unnecessary Burdens	45
Uncertainties	47
Don't Feed the Bears	49
Obstacles	51
The View	53
Muscle Cramps	55
Stuck	57
Blisters	59
The Summit	61
Monuments	63
Trail's End (or not?)	65
Author Addendum	66
Vending Machine God	69

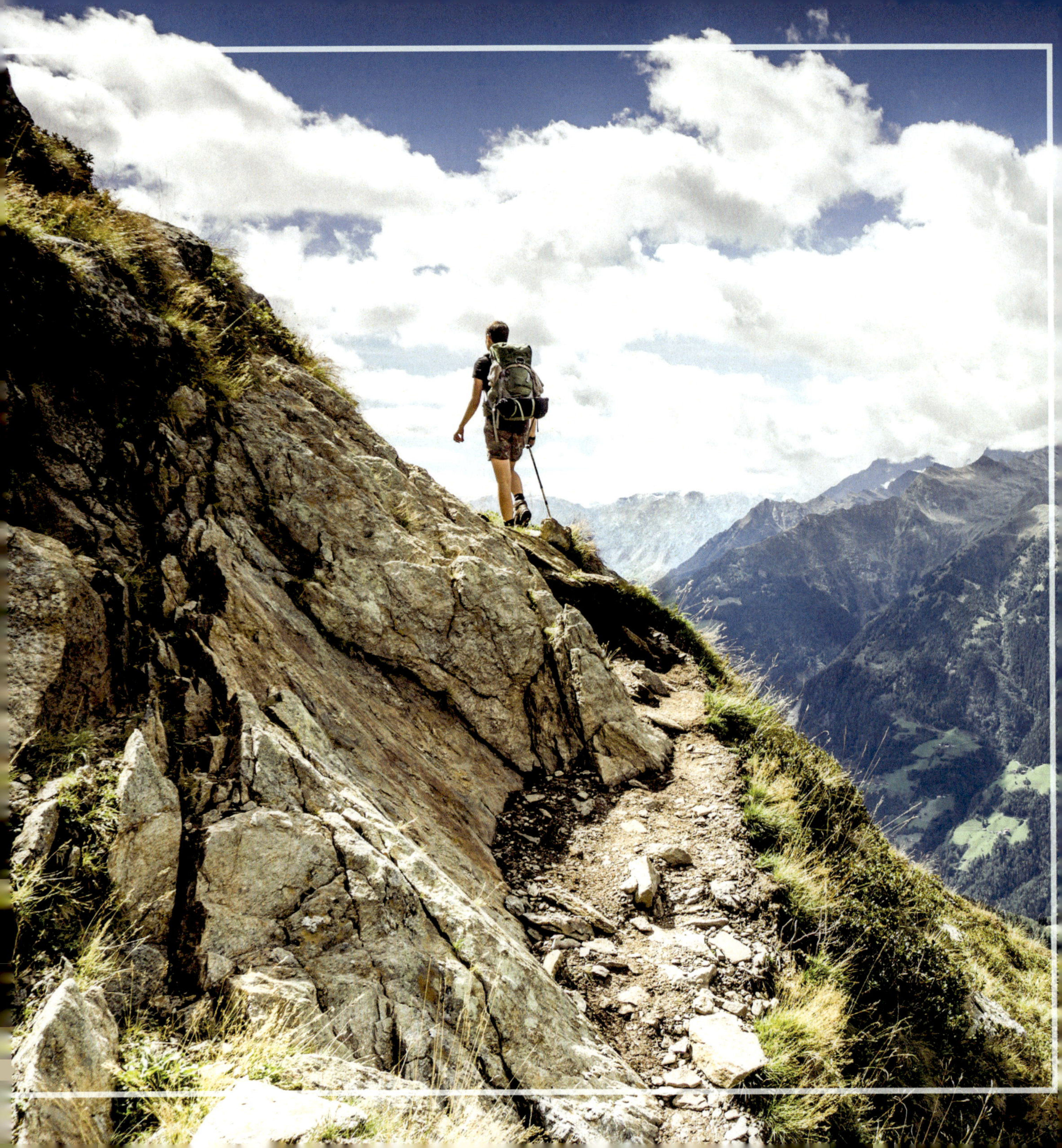

Preface

Christie: Another funeral. Once again I found myself sitting in a front pew for the fifth time in less than five years. This time it was my husband's grandma. The year before it was my husband's grandpa and then my brother-in-law Josh. Three years earlier it was two of my grandparents who died less than a month apart. I was tired of funerals. I was tired of saying good-byes and even tired of being tired. As I sat in the pew, the pastor's words faded in my ears, and in my mind I saw a mountain. It was a steep mountain with a path spiraling around it toward the top. It was a path for grievers; it was a path for me.

My path of grief has been a rugged mountain trail. Sometimes it seems I am not making any progress as I encounter the same difficult terrain repeatedly. My spiritual director, however, explained a helpful spiritual concept to me some months ago. She said although it seems I am circling around to the same place over and over, I am not really going in circles. I am *spiraling*, so that each time I come on the "same thing," I am actually meeting it at a different level—emotionally and spiritually.

Josh was only thirty-six years old. He was my husband's brother, my children's uncle, and my good friend since second grade. His cancer brought surgeries, chemotherapy, difficult talks, stolen plans for the future, tears, and the uncertainty of how everything would play out. It was all too much for my heart and mind to process. How could this have happened? I would never be the same.

As I pondered "Grief Mountain" from my funeral service pew, I knew it was more than a chance vision in my head; it was meant to take form in a book. My thoughts slowly returned to the memorial service, but later that night, I thought of Myron. He had recently lost his father and was processing his own grief, *and* he enjoyed writing. I had never thought of writing with him before, but I somehow knew we should write this together. Maybe we could help someone else in their grief by writing about what we had learned with our own.

Myron: I was in a time of transition. I knew God had something He wanted me to be working on, but I was clueless about what that might be. When Christie approached me, I felt an immediate resonance that this was what I had been waiting for.

Although my dad was eighty-three years old when he passed away, I was surprised at the profound effect his death had on me. His life had deeply formed me, and his death continues to affect me. I realize my participation in writing this book is part of the way I am processing my own grief journey.

We feel privileged to share our thoughts and experiences with you—not as experts but as fellow pilgrims on the way.

Christie Ollar and Myron Miller

Introduction

Life is an adventure with experiences to enjoy and worlds to explore. But life is also a journey with obstacles and challenges that can sometimes feel overwhelming. At times our happiness seems all too fragile. Although the details of our life journeys are unique, when confronted with grief we find ourselves on paths that share many similarities.

Grief is the sorrow or distress we experience due to a significant loss. We may experience grief from losing a job, a marriage, our health, or a loved one through death or separation. Although we may suffer many different kinds of loss, the grief process has striking similarities regardless of the type of loss we suffer.

While our discussion in this book focuses on loss through death, many of the ideas we present are transferable. At some point in time, unless we ourselves die young, someone close to us will die. We will not have chosen this difficult path of sorrow and pain, yet it will stubbornly lie before us.

The hike up Grief Mountain may seem like an unwelcome detour in life, but perhaps it can be more than an undesirable deviation. Some of us will want to avoid this demanding climb, to bypass this unwanted trail. Taking another path, however, has its own consequences. First, choosing a path of avoidance or denial has its own hiking challenges, and its own costs. Secondly, the grief path *not* travelled would have had benefits that will now be missed, lessons unlearned, and wisdom ungathered.

Sometimes, circumstances beyond our control delay our engaging the grief journey. I knew a woman whose husband died suddenly. They had three young children and the wife felt she had to be strong to help her children navigate the loss of their father. She also had to manage all the funeral arrangements, take care of the family's financial affairs, and find a new job while still continuing to do her previous family duties.

Six months after her husband's death she took a leisurely walk around a nearby lake. While strolling, she reflected on how well she had processed her grief and how unscathed she seemed to be. In that brief, unguarded moment, she was surprised to find herself suddenly sobbing uncontrollably. Her emotions that had been carefully tucked away in a closet suddenly broke free with great fervor. Her grief journey had been delayed by circumstances, but not avoided.

Although the timing may vary, we cannot decide *not* to have a loss, only which path we will take when it comes. The coin has already been flipped—living life means we will experience loss. The coin will land one of two ways; we need to call it in the air, "Heads or tails?" Grief Mountain or denial?

Climbing Grief Mountain requires both courage and submission. Courage is required because it is not an easy hike and there are many unknowns. Submission is required because we are unable to change the mountain path. By climbing, however, the path *will* change us. How might the climb affect us? What are the challenges we will face? Is there anyone who can help us (a stray Sherpa perhaps)? Where is God when we feel so alone? On the summit, what impressions might we have looking back on the path just traveled, or looking ahead to life after grief?

We invite you to some reflections gleaned from our own stories of mourning, our own hikes. Our hope is that by sharing our journeys and thoughts with you, your journeys of grief and mourning might be just a bit easier.

Will you join us? Let's go for a hike.

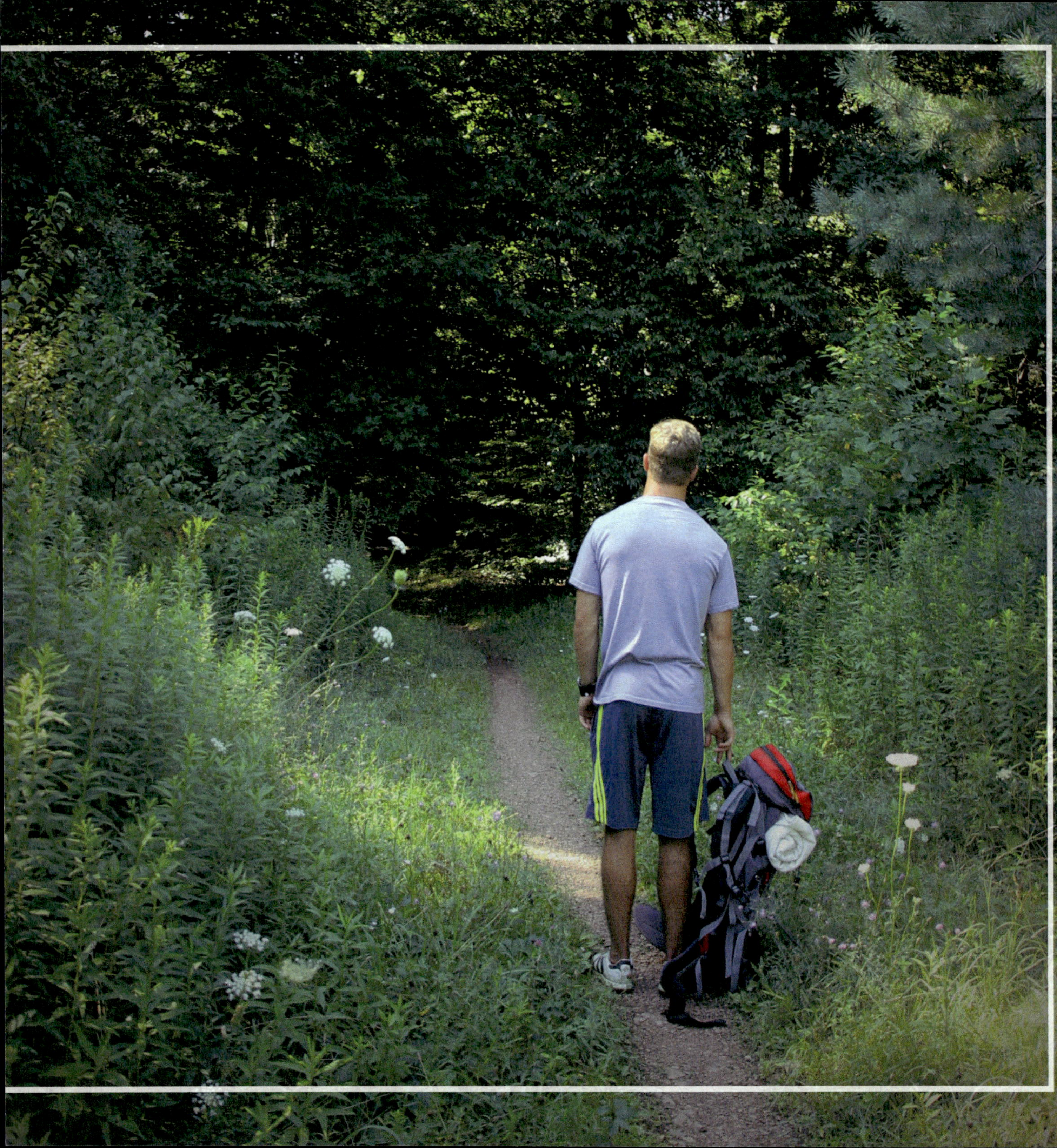

The Reluctant Hiker

Our inability to understand why tragedy has visited us may make us unenthusiastic, if not unwilling, to start the painful grief journey that lies before us. *This was so unfair. I really don't want to do this. Why has this happened to me?*

Our "Why" questions *seem* to arise out of a logical thought process. But is it logical to expect our universe to dole out blessings and difficulties fairly? Even for those of us who believe in an all-powerful God, we must admit that Scripture tells us He "sends rain [and drought] on the just and the unjust" (Matt 5:45).

So perhaps our "Why" questions arise more from our feelings than our thoughts. If this is the case, logical "head" responses to our "heart" questions about suffering and death are wrong-headed and will consistently fail to satisfy. Our need in times of mourning may be less for acquiring information than for receiving comfort. We don't need great wisdom and counsel so much as we need genuine caring and compassion.

While "Why" questions may not be very helpful, reframing our perspective with different questions that accept the reality of our present situation could prove valuable. *What can I do with where I am now? Who can walk with me and provide compassion and encouragement? When should I continue walking, and when should I stop to rest and reflect?*

While God is not the author of tragedy, He is the master redeemer of all things. God delights in taking that which seems destined to go from bad to worse, and turning it topsy-turvy to bring about good (Romans 8:28). This includes even the most horrific of events.

Myron: *Three weeks ago, my nephew, Michael Sharp (M.J.), a UN worker in the Congo (DRC), was kidnapped and then brutally killed. He was thirty-four years old. M.J. spent his last five years in the Congo. He worked to get child soldiers out of rebel militant groups and to find peaceful ways to get militants to lay down their arms and return to their homes. He loved the Congolese people and his deep desire was to be able to help them.*

How does one ever make sense of M.J.'s death for his mother, father, and two sisters? No matter how much "good" might come out of this, on a feeling level, it's not enough—we just want our M.J. back. While our heads may logically concede the possibility God can bring good out of devastation, can we trust in God's goodness even when we can't see or even imagine any good purpose?

The positive potential for the grief process is rarely seen when we are mired in the experience. It is more often a surprise seen in hindsight. Admittedly, however, sometimes we are *never* able to grasp any good consequences. In these situations, though perhaps reluctant, can we still trust God enough to start walking the grief path before us?

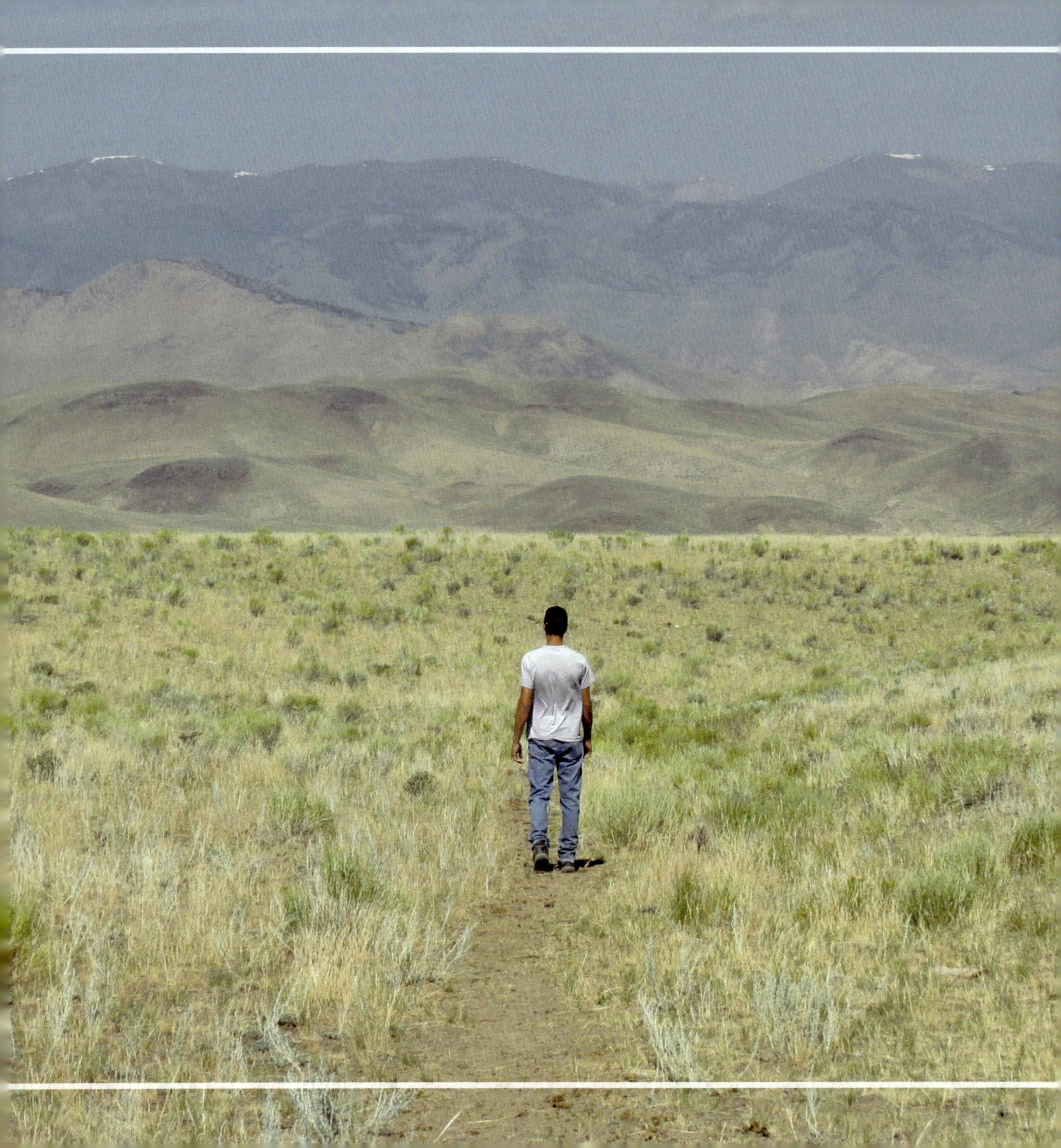

New Terrain

Sometimes we hike trails well known to us. They feel comfortable, like sliding into an old pair of shoes. Other times, though, we are hiking uncharted territory, where we feel like a lumberjack who finds himself sitting at a spinning wheel. "What do I do now?" Grief often leads us into unknown terrain requiring frequent adjustments along the way. Life does not stop for us just because our world has turned upside down.

When a loved one dies, we suddenly need to adjust to a new reality. In *A Grief Observed*, C.S. Lewis describes the scope of the changes: "Her absence is like the sky, spread over everything." At dinnertime we may pull out their plate and suddenly realize it is no longer needed. We hit speed dial to share some good news and then remember our call will go unanswered. These moments can be crushing. Loneliness sweeps over us, and we sluggishly try to recalculate what to do next. Over time, as we adjust to their continued absence, the pain will lessen. Meanwhile, someone else might enjoy the dinner invitation or the phone call.

Losing a loved one also involves losing the roles they filled. They may have been the driver, the cook, the banker, or the computer person in the family. We find ourselves needing to learn how to fill those functions. If our primary identity was being a mother and we lost our child, or being a husband and we lost our wife, the way we view ourselves must be redefined.

Adjusting to loss does not mean we can expect other persons to fill the shoes of our loved one. Each person is different and has a special place in our lives. When missing one who was dear to us, it is common to find ourselves expecting another friend or family member to fill the void. But pushing harder will not make a round peg fit into a square hole. One person cannot replace another. To expect someone to do so is unfair to them and frustrating for us.

Instead, we can nurture new relationships and strengthen old ones. We can lean on our friends, lean on our family, and lean on our God—they all want to help us through this time of pain. While we are in uncharted territory, we need not hike this new terrain alone.

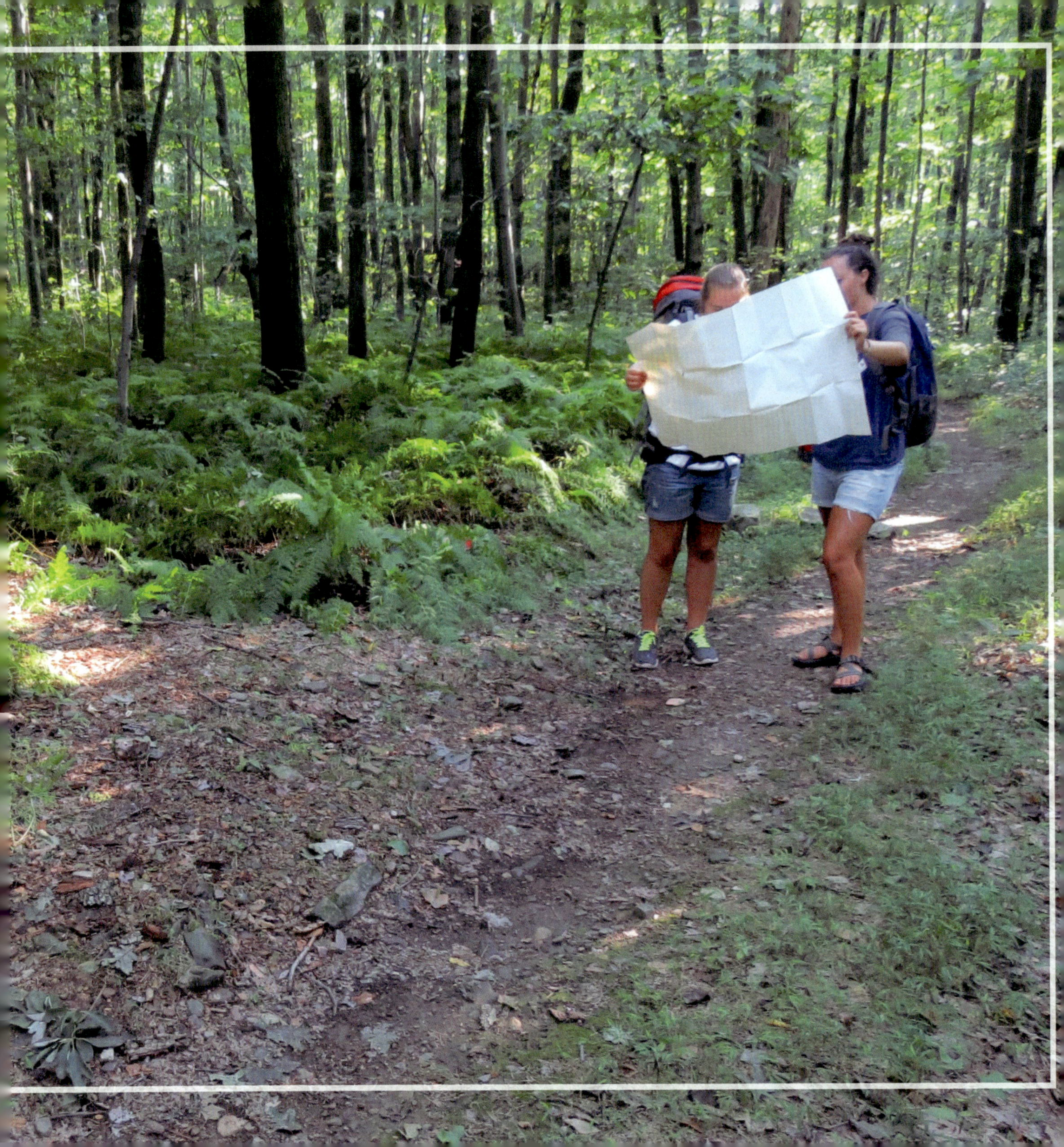

Lost

Although the grief hike may be a new experience for many of us, it is surprising that we still imagine we can find our own way. Since you are reading this, I have to wonder, *How's that going for you?* Unfortunately, there are no maps to chart out our grief path, and traditional compass needles often spin in confusion. Landmarks we have relied on in the past are suddenly hard to recognize. Dazed and disoriented, we stop still in our tracks as the realization that we are lost slowly dawns on us.

Each trail of grief and sorrow is unique. No one has ever travelled our specific path, so being disoriented and lost is a normal expectation. Even the great frontiersman Daniel Boone, when asked if he ever had trouble finding his way in the woods, replied: "I've never been lost, but I was once bewildered for three days." Being disoriented, confused and bewildered puts us in good company with the rest of humanity.

Ironically, knowing ourselves to be lost helps by being the starting point for our reorientation. The "You Are Here" arrow on the map of Grief Mountain sometimes points to "Lost." Realizing we are disoriented or lost prompts us to ask: *What was helpful to me when I needed guidance in the past? Who might be able to help me? How can I reorient myself?*

Often, those who have already hiked Grief Mountain have helped mark the way for us. A cairn is a human-made stack of stones used as a trail marker. Some modern trails may have trail blazes in the form of spray paint on the trees. Our thoughtful predecessors on the trail labored to help make our journey a bit easier. Pride should not keep us from seeking help. We should use any and all assistance available to us.

While family and friends can be helpful when feeling lost, some persons are more helpful than others. Avoiding certain friends on the grief trail may be a wise decision. God, however, is a friend we can always count on. Nonetheless, we find it hard to turn to God when we are angry with Him for allowing all this woe. Yet isn't it a bit foolish to spurn the Mapmaker when we are lost and directionally challenged?

When lost, we lack direction, but we still possess the commodity of time. Time can be an unexpected aid on this journey. We need to be patient with ourselves and realize that the grieving process cannot be rushed—time is our friend. If uncertain how to proceed, we can use the time to rest, to assess ourselves, and to let others help us. *Where have we been, and what have we learned? How are we doing?* We should not only listen to messages from our minds, but also those coming from our bodies and emotions. While we may be *lost* in one sense, we can use the time to *find* other things of great value, like rest, strength, encouragement, and insights.

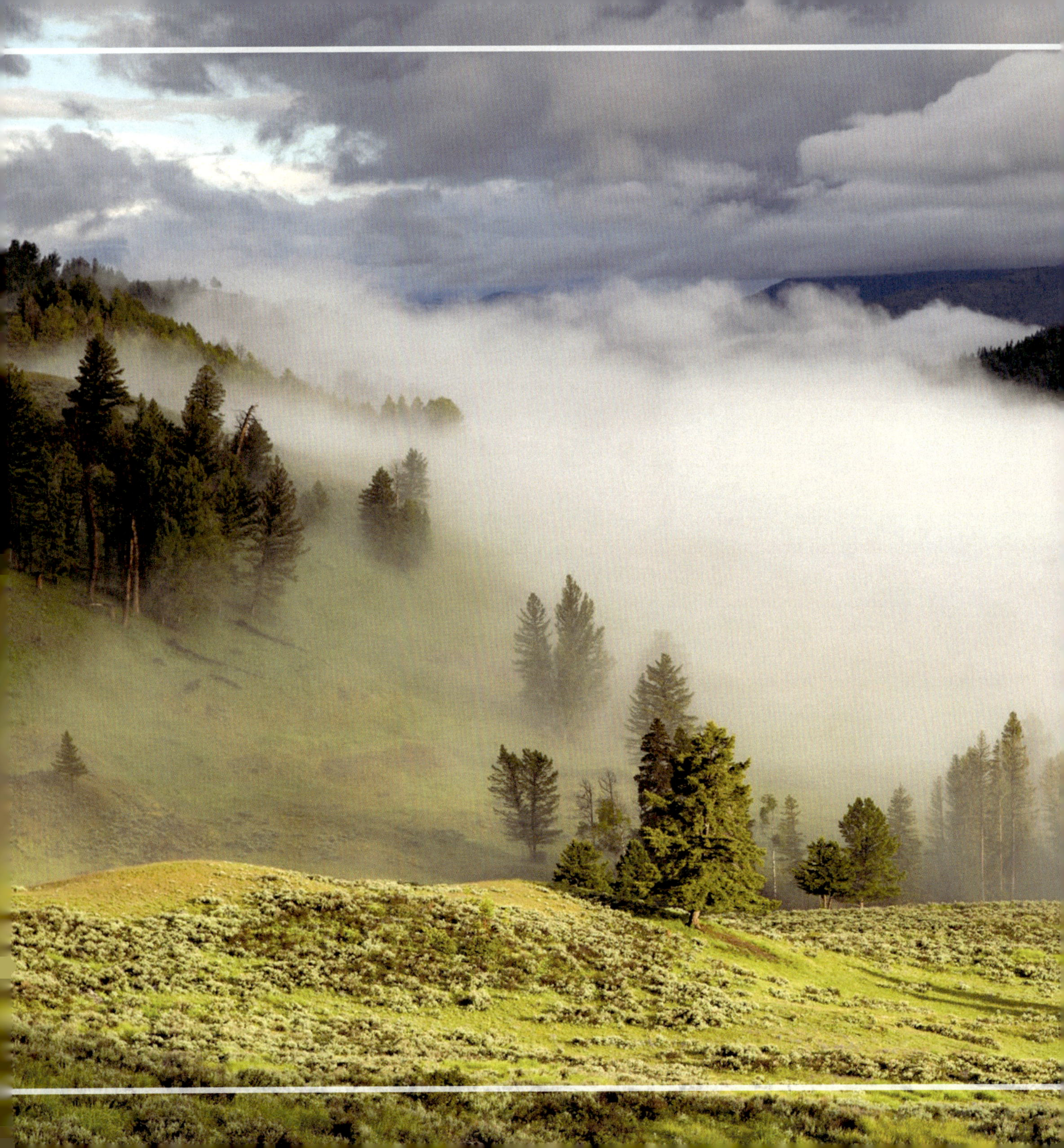

Fog

When water vapor is in the skies, we call it clouds. Nothing is more beautiful than these white, cotton masses migrating across a canvas of blue. However, when that same mist descends to the level of our mountain trail, we call it fog, and it morphs from a natural beauty into a navigational burden.

With the process of grief, fogginess can affect our minds. We have difficulty concentrating on common tasks and find ourselves embarrassingly forgetful. Simple responsibilities like reading instructions or balancing our checkbooks seem impossible to complete. We finish a job only later to discover we didn't do it correctly. We did the laundry without putting detergent in the washing machine. We discover the cereal box in the refrigerator and the milk in the cupboard.

It may also be difficult to control our emotions. We find ourselves crying at the drop of a hat or snapping at an unsuspecting friend for a trivial offense. Recurrent dreams about our absent loved one are common, and it is not unusual for some to think they hear their loved one's voice.

Are we going crazy? No, we are not going off the deep end. Our dear one has recently passed away, and the emotional stress, sleepless nights, depression, and worry can send our brains into temporary shock. This is only transient, and our minds will gradually improve as we continue our grief journey. We just need to take one step at a time and one day at a time.

Difficulty concentrating may make us more accident-prone. Extra care should be taken with driving, cooking, or operating machinery. We should avoid making major decisions until our minds are working more clearly.

The Old Testament prophet Jeremiah wrote an entire book of the Bible filled with his passionate laments. Yet he declared it was God's love that gave him hope and kept him from being consumed by his grief. "But this I call to mind, and therefore I have hope: the steadfast love of the LORD never ceases; his mercies never come to an end;" (Lamentations 3:21-22). We *will* eventually make it through. In time the fog will lift.

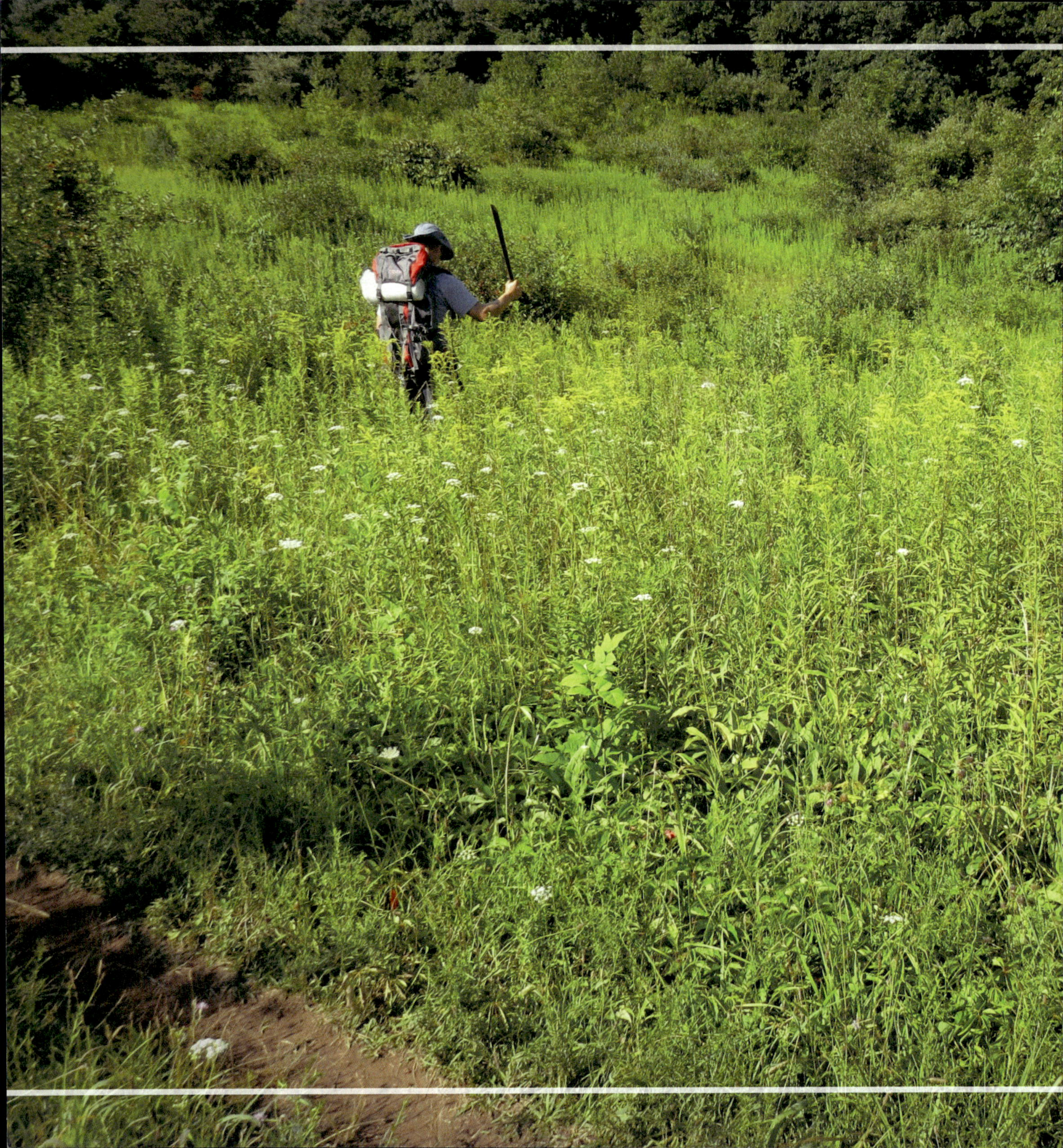

Bushwhacking

Bushwhacking is hiking through an area where no path exists. Hiking involves a whole new set of dangers when we get off the well-worn trail. The main trail is clear of poison ivy and hidden tree roots that might trip us up. Snakes are clearly visible and easily sidestepped on the bare path. The main path also has trail markers that make it harder to get lost. These advantages are missing when one goes bushwhacking.

Nonetheless, some of us hikers think we are immune to alleged off-trail hazards. *The shortest distance between two points is a straight line, and by golly we are going for it!* We can bypass a lot of this grief and pain; let's go for it. This attitude involves pride that assumes we know what is best and that we need not travel a path we don't like and didn't choose.

Sometimes we get off the grief trail because the sorrow and pain are so severe we are unable to bear it—*I'm out of here!* Wanting to run away from grief is very understandable. Making our own path gives us the illusion of having control and *not* having pain. But emotional bushwhacking doesn't really get rid of the pain. If grief is not expressed through sorrow and tears, it may manifest itself as anger, impatience, or depression.

Feeling sadness and heartache is actually a good thing. Early on in the aftermath of losing someone dear to us, it is common to be numb, feeling almost nothing. This emotional shock can serve to shield us from being overwhelmed by too much pain. Truly dealing with our feelings, however, requires experiencing them. We can only heal what we feel. Give yourself permission to feel the pain of grief. This is normal and healthy, and part of the path to healing

Using the bushwhacking technique may seem to let us avoid the hard work of grieving. Talking about our gloomy feelings is a difficult, awkward, and vulnerable task. It may seem that if we just refuse to admit we have sad feelings, perhaps they won't really exist.

This is like not taking a temperature reading to avoid having a fever. In the short run, this seems good—no fever. In the long run, however, it is not so good—undiagnosed pneumonia. The grief trail exists and leads where it does for a reason. Bushwhacking to find "shortcuts" is nothing more than false advertising. It won't really make the journey quicker or easier. Stay on the trail.

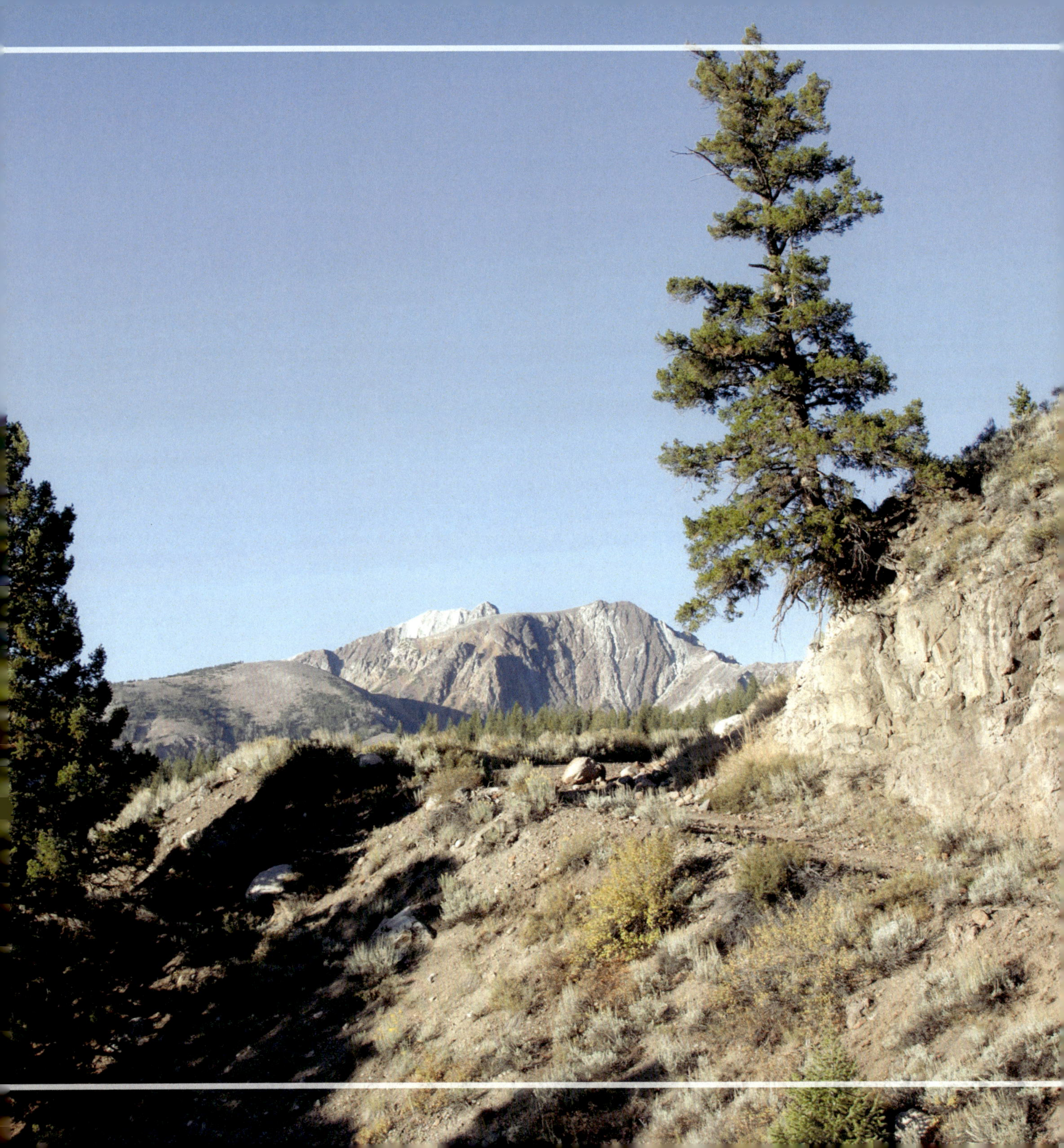

Loss of Control

As hikers on a new trail, we need to learn to give up the myth that we are in control of what happens. We cannot prearrange what lies around the next bend, how many steep inclines we will need to climb, what animals and plants we will see, how many obstacles may lie in our way, or what injuries we may sustain.

Tragedy is a blatant reminder that we have limited control in our lives. Responding to this new awareness of our vulnerability can cause us to overreact to ordinary circumstances. Fear or even panic may be triggered by mundane daily occurrences. The smell of smoke doesn't necessarily mean there's a forest fire; it may just be a campfire. The sound of sirens or a helicopter might trigger a sense of intense anxiety. A lump under our arm or experiencing a common ailment finds us preparing for the inevitable chemotherapy and hospice consultation. When someone we are expecting doesn't arrive on time, we instantly fear they've been in a terrible accident.

When we lose someone we love, our instinct is to tighten our grip on those we still have. We want to control things so we aren't hurt again. The desire to maintain control may also manifest itself as blaming others or ourselves.

Attaching blame provides us with an answer. Our minds need to somehow make sense of an irrational tragedy. Blaming someone, no matter how unreasonable that may be, gives us an answer; it offers a *reason* for what happened. Having some kind of answer to cling to provides hope that we can prevent a similar devastation in the future. If we just handle this differently the next time, we can avoid a repeat disaster. Having an answer, no matter how feeble it may be, offers a way for us to feel we still have control in our lives.

The unsettling truth is that we are *not* in control. Although we can make good or bad decisions, the results are often outside our control. While it is impossible to have complete control, it is possible to have peace and hope in the midst of uncertainties and even tragedies.

As Christians, our peace and hope is in the resurrected Jesus Christ. He is our peace because we know that no matter what happens, he loves us and will be with us. His victory over death is our hope for the same resurrection. This sure hope can bring perspective to our journeys of mourning. As we trust our triune God, we are able to surrender our white-knuckle grip that vainly struggles for a control that is impossible to attain.

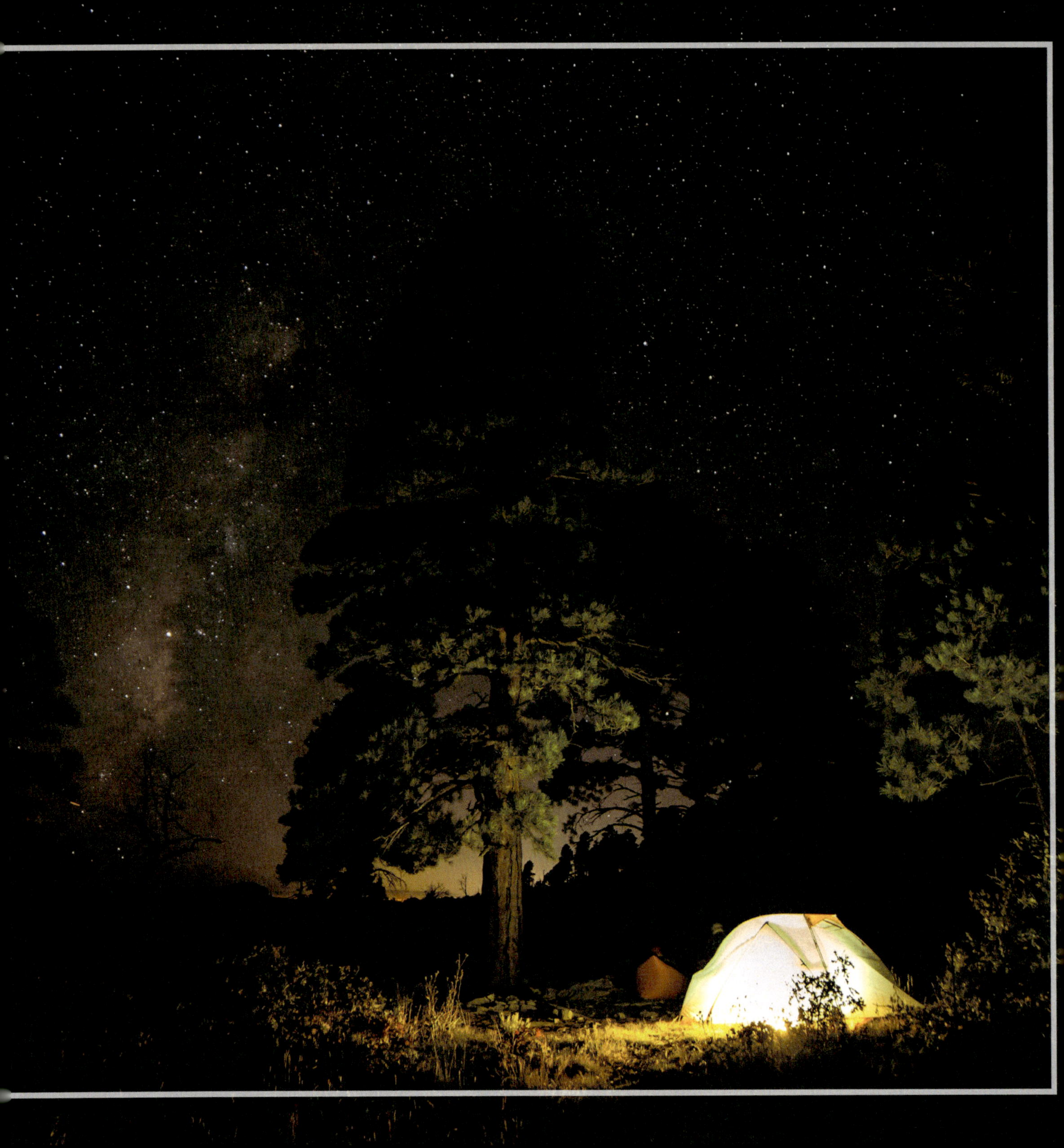

Darkness

One thing no hiker wants to do is hike the trail at night. Hiking has enough challenges when we can *see* what's ahead. Darkness adds a whole new set of fears. Does the trail go to the right or to the left? Is there a sheer drop-off or a boulder in front of me? Is that scurrying noise from a possum or a skunk? Darkness quickly turns a carefree hike into a scary trek with hidden dangers and anxious unknowns.

We learned the simple remedy for darkness as a child—turn on the light switch or the flashlight, or at least get a night-light. Unfortunately, we have carried our childhood solutions of night-lights and flashlights into adulthood. We view grief as a form of darkness, and our reflex response is to get out of the darkness and into the light ASAP.

But does God abandon us in the darkness? Is there nothing God might want to teach us in the dark of night? Before we turn on the lights, perhaps we should sit in the darkness, try to sense His presence, and strain to hear His soft voice in the silent darkness. I think most of us would have to admit we have learned some vital lessons in the dark. Yet we tend to whisper this truth, fearful that if God hears us He may kindly "bless" us with *more* tragedy. While fears and dangers might lurk in the darkness, beauty and wisdom can also dwell there.

Our house has an outdoor night guard light that comes on automatically when it gets dark. While the light helps us feel safer, an unintended consequence is that our view of the stars is diluted. I have a friend, an amateur astronomer, who has made several trips to interior Australia where the lack of light contamination gives him an amazingly unspoiled view of the virgin night sky. He is willing to spend a lot of time and money to get that uniquely clear view we so casually discard.

It made me wonder, to what ends are we willing to go for a clearer view of what God might want to show us, to better hear what He is trying to tell us? Dare we linger where things seem dark to glimpse the spiritual stars God has for us? Although God may at times seem distant, we know He is with us even in the dark pain of grief. In fact, C. S. Lewis says God often uses pain to His advantage, as a "megaphone to rouse a deaf world."

Scripture tells us it is God's desire ultimately to redeem all things. Grief is a result of our fallen world, but one day grief will be no more, and God "will wipe away every tear" (Revelation 21:4). I believe even now, God is not defeated by grief. God walks the dark path of grief with us, and as we travel together, He teaches us deep truths. We see more clearly the things that truly matter in life. These truths, birthed in pain and darkness, will elude those who live charmed lives of ease in the constant light of day.

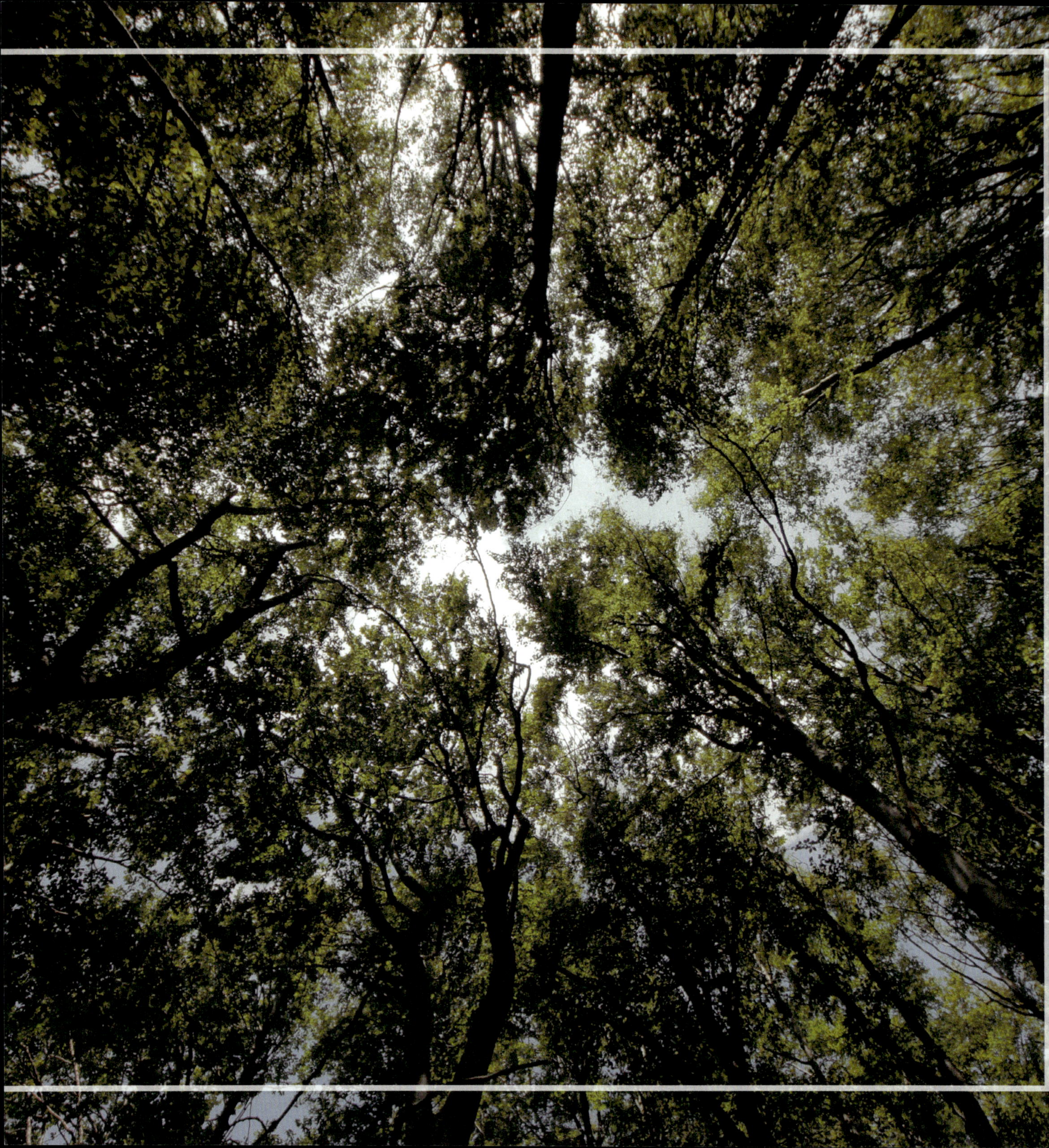

Vertigo

For a successful hike, our minds, bodies, and emotions need to be functioning well. Our bodies need to be strong, rested, hydrated and fed, and we need good balance. Dizziness on a dangerous trail could spell disaster. When we suffer an attack of vertigo, it seems as though the world is moving unpredictably, when actually it is we who have the issue.

On the grief trail, there will be times when we experience emotional vertigo. If we had only one emotion to deal with at a time, the situation might be workable. The reality, however, is that we are experiencing multiple emotions, and some of them seem contradictory. The spinning begins.

When someone close to us dies, we naturally experience **sadness** at our loss, and **pain** for which there seems to be no remedy. British author J. K. Rowling describes grief as "caring so much you feel as though you will bleed to death with the pain of it."

Although hard to admit, it is common to be **angry** with God. After all, God allowed this death and refused to intervene miraculously to heal our loved one or prevent the tragedy. Surprisingly, we might also find ourselves angry with the deceased person: *Why weren't they more careful? Why didn't they take better care of themselves? How could they leave me alone to cope with life?*

Another common emotion is **guilt**: *I should have reminded them to drive carefully. I should have made them go to the doctor sooner. If only I had....* We may also have survivor's guilt: *It should have been me instead of them.*

Although it is difficult to admit, a sense of **relief** is also common. Their suffering is over, and if they were believers, we probably have a sense of comfort that they are in the presence of our loving God. If we were a caregiver for them, we will also have a sense of relief that our difficult task of going to see them regularly, our loss of sleep, and the duty of caring for their physical, emotional and spiritual needs is now over.

If our relationship was a good one, we will also feel **gratitude** for what we had with them. Nonetheless, their absence produces a vacancy in our lives and **loneliness** in the pit of our souls.

This whirlwind of emotions (sadness, pain, anger, guilt, relief, gratitude, and loneliness) can be difficult to process. A few of these emotions are probably perceived as "positive" and others as "negative." Some of these feelings are directed toward ourselves, some toward others, some toward God; and some of these feelings are free-floating, in search of a target. One of the hallmarks of grief is the presence of conflicting emotions. Although grief is the normal emotional reaction to loss, normal does not mean easy. While emotional vertigo can be very distressing, remember this too will pass.

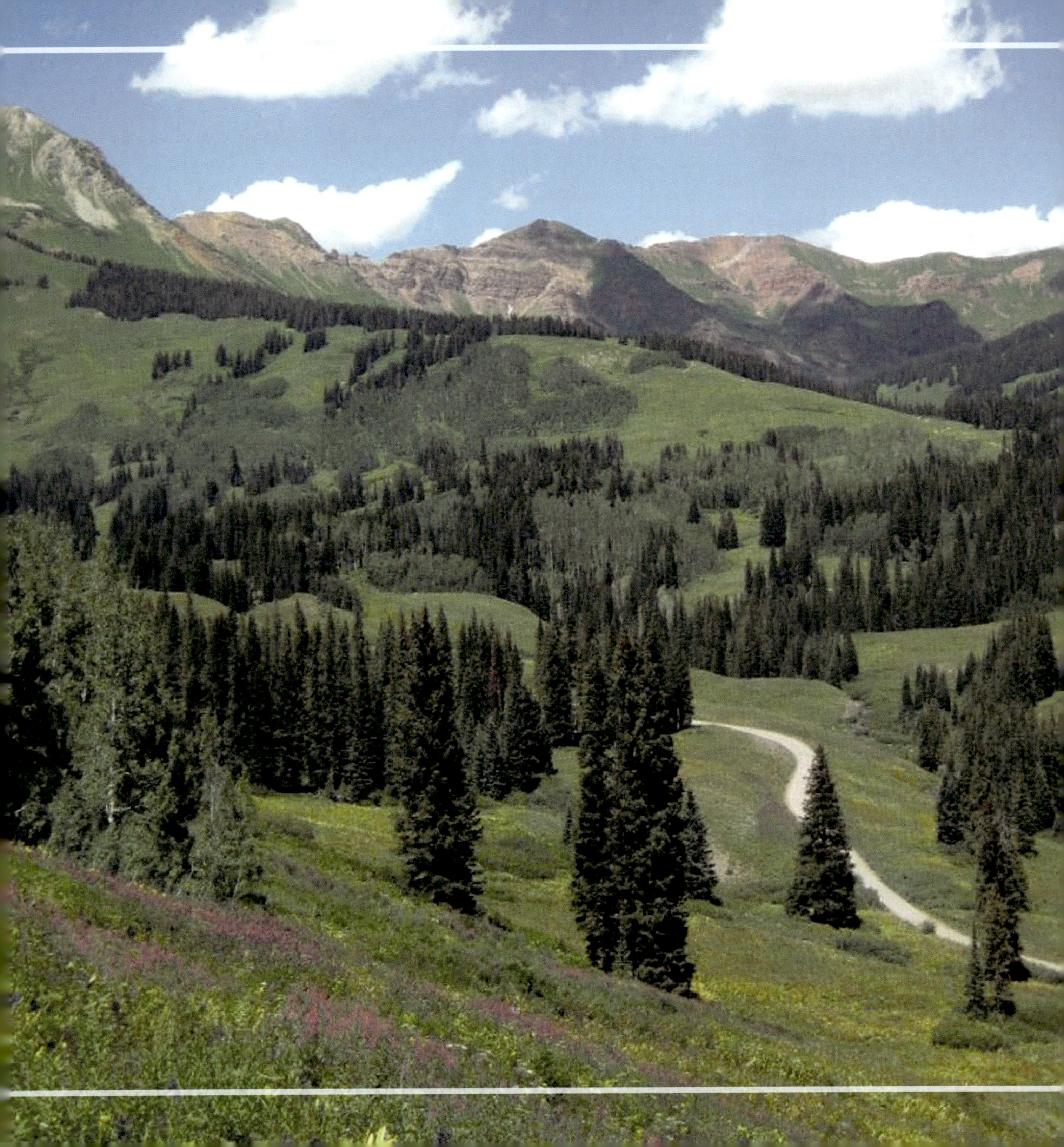

The Trail Traveled

We hikers often look back on the trail behind us. It is nice to see the progress we have made and to remember past trail experiences. It also gives us a chance to catch our breath and rest our tired muscles after hiking a particularly steep or rugged stretch.

However, if we keep our gaze on the trail already traveled for too long, we will never see the breathtaking scene around the next bend. Or we miss the newborn fawn taking its first wobbly steps just over the crest of the hill.

Revisiting memories of our loved ones, like looking back on the trail, can have pros and cons. Our recollections can be a source of comfort, joy, and healing, or they can cause sadness, anxiety, and misery.

As we reflect on our past experiences with our departed loved one, we often experience warm feelings of nostalgia that quicken our hearts and lead to a desire to relive those past experiences. Good memories are part of the joy of our lives. Scottish novelist J. M. Barrie said, "God gave us memory so that we might have roses in December." We can fondly remember the fragrance of our loved one long after they are gone.

While it is easy to see the benefit of warm memories, it is hard to separate them from the ever-present, painful sense of loss. Hence, we might try to avoid past memories altogether. We can deny they exist, ignore them if they show up, or distract ourselves with other issues. Although counterintuitive, allowing ourselves to reflect on the good and the bad is often the best approach. Remembering is a normal part of the mourning process, and trying to avoid it will only prolong the time needed for healing to occur. Our mind's memories can be a healing balm for our heart's injuries.

While visiting past memories can be helpful, living in the past is not. We need to live in the present, where new memories are being made. Living fully in the present helps provide strength and courage to move forward into the future, where we can find goodness, joy, and beauty.

The trail traveled is paradoxically complex. It is a source of sadness, joy, wounds, and healing. While it is sometimes helpful to look backward, we need to remember that the rest of our lives lies in front of us.

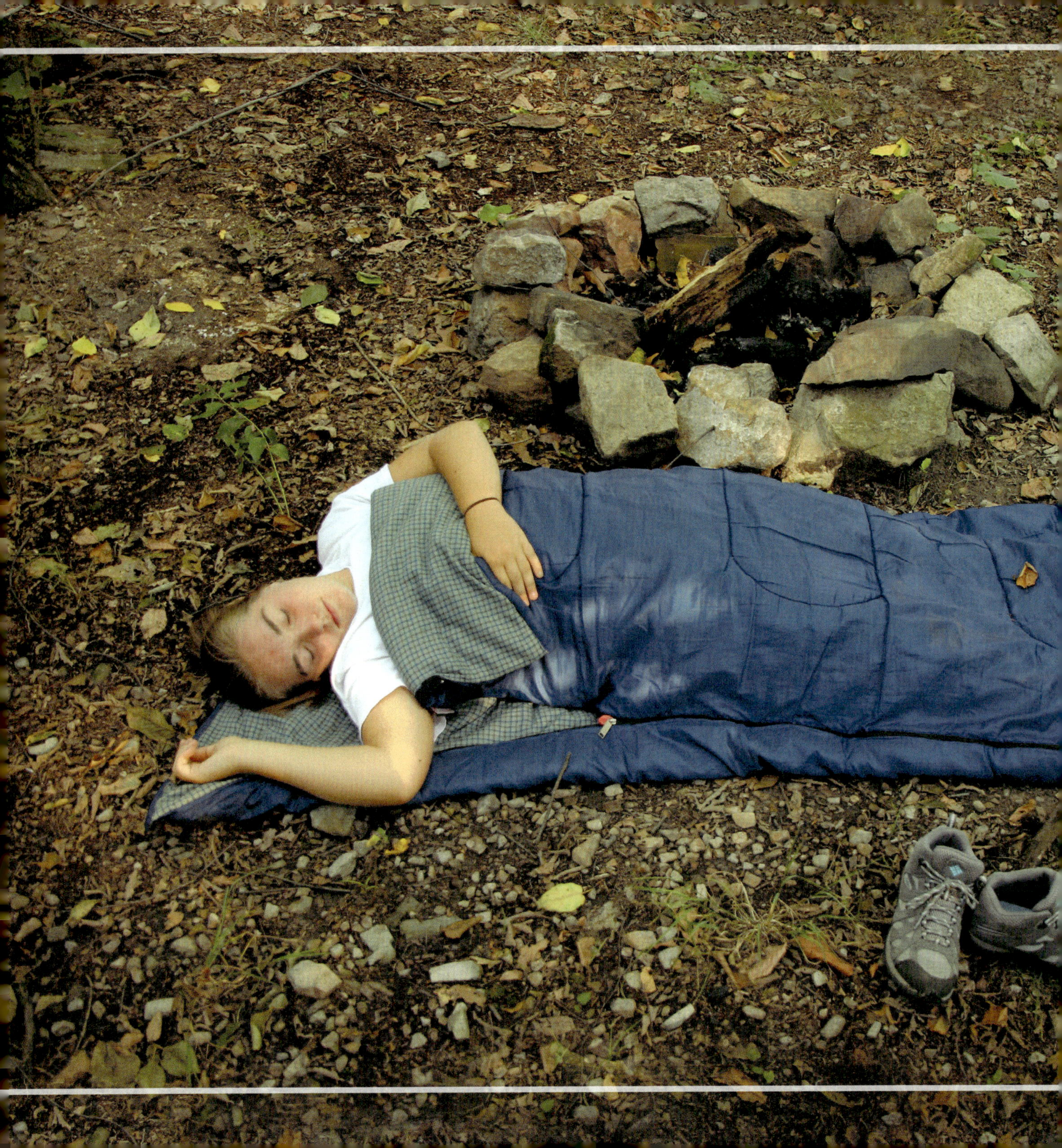

Fatigue

Hiking Grief Mountain takes more energy than anyone can imagine. Virtually all hikers at some point get to the place where we feel incapable of taking even one more step. The hike is physically, emotionally, mentally, and spiritually exhausting. Some mornings, just getting out of our sleeping bags to face the day requires a herculean effort. Will the day ahead of me be as hard as yesterday? Rest is often appropriate, yet sometimes the best response to fatigue is just to keep going. The strength to continue may come from a variety of sources.

We can begin by realizing we need to eat. Even though we may not be hungry, our bodies require food to keep going. And although being alone may seem easier, spending time with close friends can be rejuvenating. Faith can be another source of strength when we feel too weary to walk.

If we blamed and then abandoned God, we need to realize that served no good purpose. We should talk to Him even if only to vent our anger. God can take our complaining, and He yearns to strengthen us on our journey. When the Old Testament psalmist's own strength was inadequate, he turned to his God: "God is our refuge and strength, a very present help in trouble" (Psalm 46:1). Even if faith has not previously been a part of our life journeys, we can be open to that changing.

Sometimes, our response to fatigue must be to rest. We need to realize again the importance of being kind to ourselves—eat some chocolate, hold a newborn baby, watch a movie, or enjoy a bubble bath. What we are going through is the emotional equivalent of running back-to-back marathons. When our last ounce of energy has been spent, a critical attitude toward ourselves is not helpful. Fatigue is not our fault. We need to treat ourselves with gentleness, care, and lots of nurturing patience.

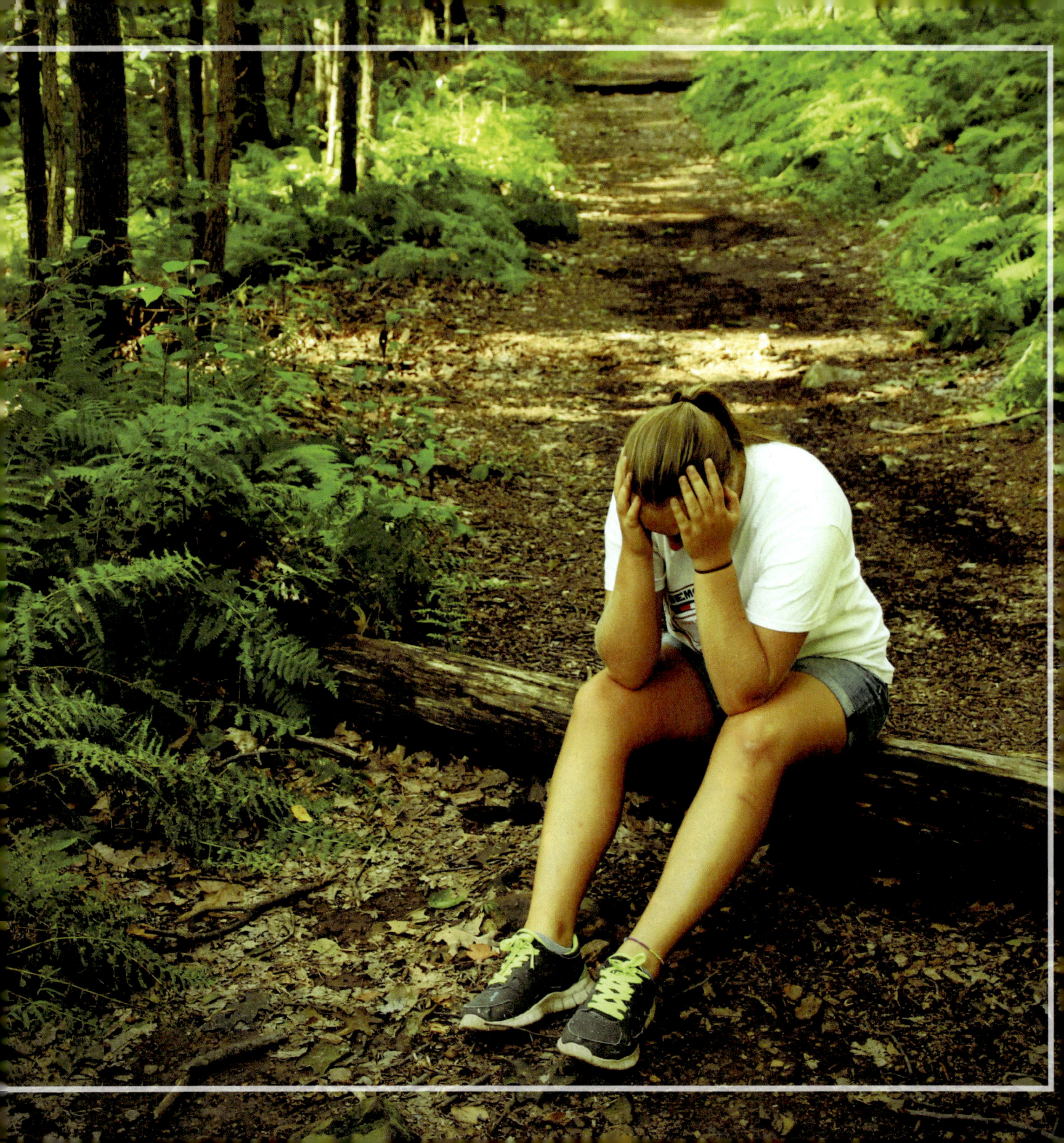

Despair

Whether one is hiking or in difficult life situations, it is common to experience a feeling of hopelessness—despair. *My knees are sore and giving out; I ate all my food; my water bottle's empty; I think I'm lost; it's cold, and now it's starting to rain. I can't take it anymore!* When we get to this place, despair makes a home somewhere between our solar plexus and our aching heart.

Few persons go through the process of grieving without periods of despair. We have lost someone we loved, and no words can describe our anguish. God (the perceived culprit) seems nowhere to be found. The darkness and deep sadness seem too much to bear, and we have turned over every stone in our desperate search for hope.

Myron: *My nephew, M.J., was kidnapped on March 12 of this year. During the next two weeks, our family and thousands of others across the country prayed that he would somehow be found alive. Two weeks later his body was found in a shallow grave in the jungles of the Congo (DRC).*

How could this be? Was God asleep at his post? Does prayer make any difference? Is God really good? Why is there pain, evil, suffering, and death? I sobbed. I yelled at God in anger, clearly laying out all the obvious reasons He was wrong for allowing this to happen. I clung doggedly to my faith in God, a parachute that refused to open.

When God seems distant and we have no desire for prayer, we need not fear losing our faith. Instead, we are probably experiencing the dark emptiness of sorrow. Reminding ourselves of what we have always known about God's unchanging, persistent love may be helpful during these times. Joseph Bayly once said, "Don't forget in the darkness what you learned in the light." God is good. God is loving and merciful. He is faithful and compassionate.

Promises from Scripture can also be reassuring during these times. "For I am convinced that neither death nor life, … height, nor depth, nor any other created thing, will be able to separate us from the love of God, which is in Christ Jesus our Lord" (Romans 8:38-39). The validity of our faith and the reality of God's love are not based on our feelings but on the truth of God's word and His promises (Psalm 119:81, 114).

Each day has dawn, noon, dusk and night. Each year has spring, summer, fall, and winter. These are visible realities that none would deny. While pain, suffering, and death are just as visible and inevitable, we still cry out: *How can this be?* The writer of Ecclesiastes reminds us of this inconvenient truth, "There is a time for everything … a time to be born and a time to die …" (3:1-4).

That which is true in the observable world around us is also true in our emotional and spiritual world—after the night comes the dawn. We cannot experience the morning light without first going through the darkness. Despair is not the end of our story. As we wait with but a frayed thread of faith, that truth will dawn on us. Our parachute will open in time.

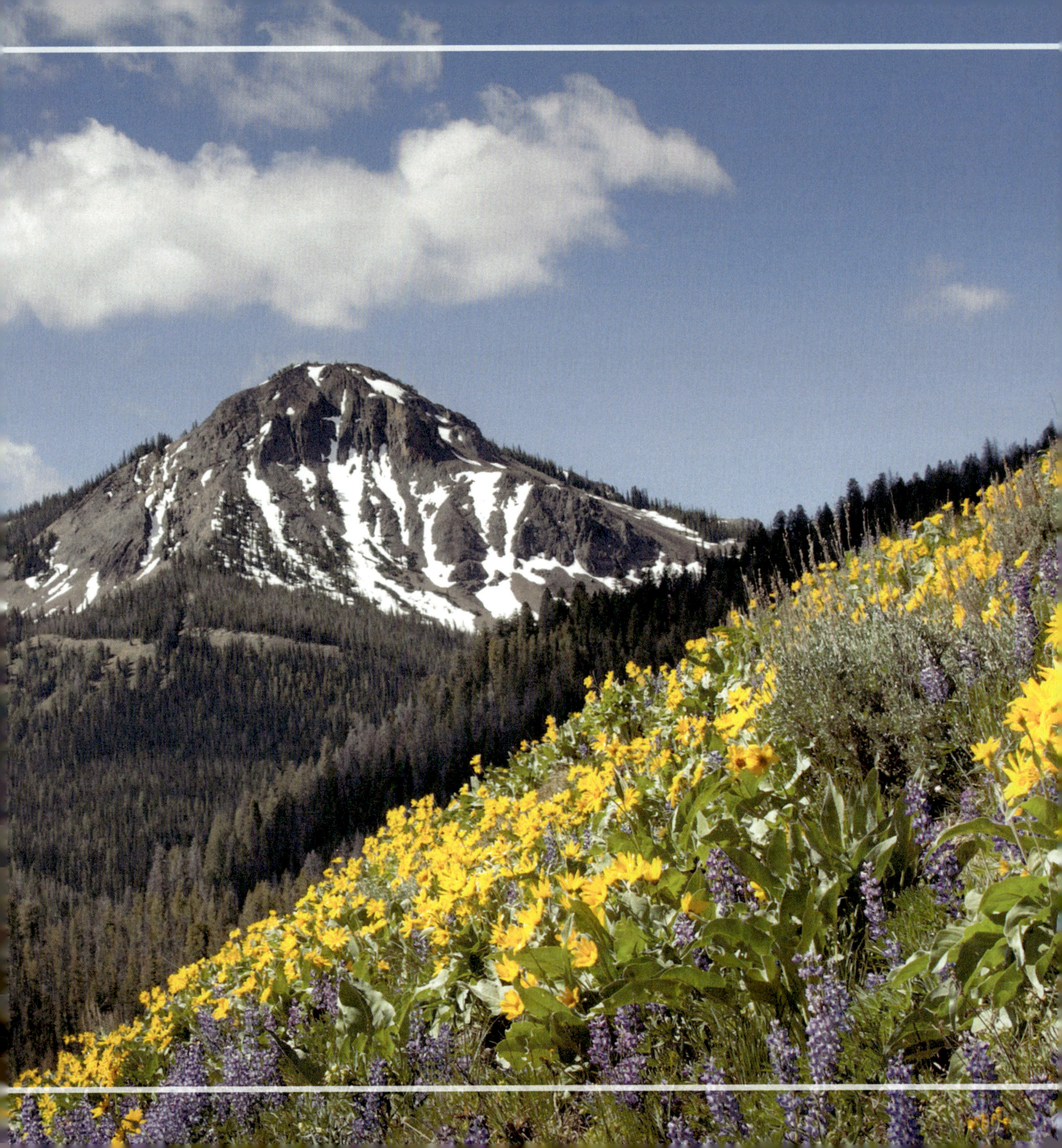

A Clearing

The journey has been difficult, but finally around the next bend is the welcome sight of a clearing. Sunlight falls on a meadow of flowers with the promise of rest from the rigors of our journey. Sitting on an old stump provides the opportunity to rest while having a drink of cool water and munching on some trail mix.

The grief journey is extremely tiring, causing emotional, physical, and spiritual fatigue. It is essential to replenish our depleted reserves so we can continue our journey. As we begin to heal, we are once again able to experience hope and joy.

After weeks or even months of unrelenting grief, a pause in the persistent oppression of sorrow may seem unsettling. When a break occurs, we may feel guilty for an apparent return to normalcy. This is no cause for shame, though, since feeling joy does not mean we have forgotten our loved one. Instead, it is just a foretaste of spring in the winter of our grief journey.

Clearings serve to remind us we are seeking something more, since our life journey will not always be a grief trek. There comes a time when we will need to decide to let go of the pain, so we can grab hold of the rest of our lives. It is important to give ourselves permission to see good things around us, to laugh, to dream, and to hope. Life contains beauty, rest and leisure. Clearings are foretastes of these joys of life and serve to rekindle our hope for experiencing them more fully.

One might mistake clearings for the end of the journey, but these glades are only rest stops. Nonetheless, clearings do become more commonplace as the hike up Grief Mountain continues. Enjoy the clearings for what they are—brief breathers on a difficult trail.

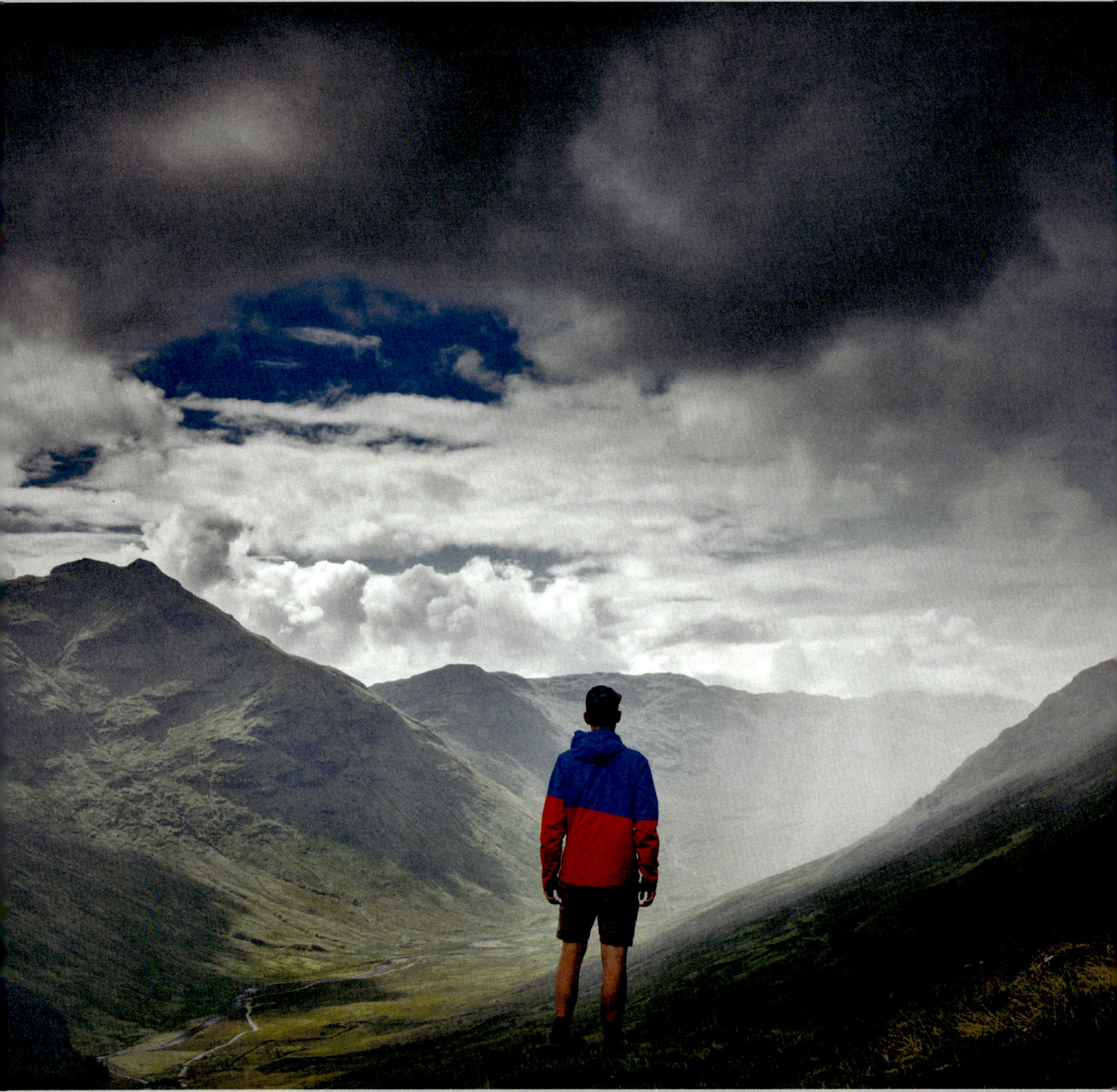

Storms

At times we notice progress being made on our path of grief. We are learning how to hike through the pain, and some days seem nearly normal. But storms can come up fast on Grief Mountain. As the rain pelts our skin, we are reminded that things are *not* really okay. Our loved one is still painfully and irrevocably gone. The storm clouds rapidly engulf us, and once again the sun, blue sky, and all good things are hidden from sight.

While it is hard not to be discouraged, stormy weather is to be expected on our trail of mourning. Many things can trigger these storms. A song on the radio, winter's first snowfall, a picture, a date on the calendar, or a familiar smell may precipitate an unexpected squall. We hear our loved one's name in casual conversation, and suddenly we find ourselves gasping for air as though drowning.

There is often a subtly critical attitude toward openly showing our emotions. Yet we cannot think our way through the grief process—we must feel our way through it. Our feelings are more than just emotional thermometers. They are also pressure gauges and healing conduits. Our feelings can give us helpful information that informs our minds and directs our actions. But if we suppress our feelings, we are unable to heal or learn from them.

Just as rain helps relieve the heavy clouds of their water burden, so tears can help relieve our heavy weight of grief. Crying tears helps to purge and cleanse our emotional debris. Studies have shown that tears actually help eliminate stress hormones in our bodies and help improve our sense of well-being. Each time we cry, we release a little more of our pain and we experience a little more healing. Tears help heal our emotions and restore our spirits like the mountain rains refresh the flowers along the trail.

Unfortunately, our culture (and sometimes our friends) may encourage us to have a "stiff upper lip" and to exercise self-restraint. Ironically, it may be more helpful if they would give us permission to cry. Crying is often a sign of strength, not weakness. Tears are a symbol of authenticity, not impending breakdown. Crying is not only "okay"; it is good, healthy, and normal.

Myron: *After the death of my nephew, the first time my sister and I communicated by phone, we could do little more than crying into our phones together—1,300 miles apart, our tears mingled. Don't be afraid to cry. Before storms can clear, the rain must fall.*

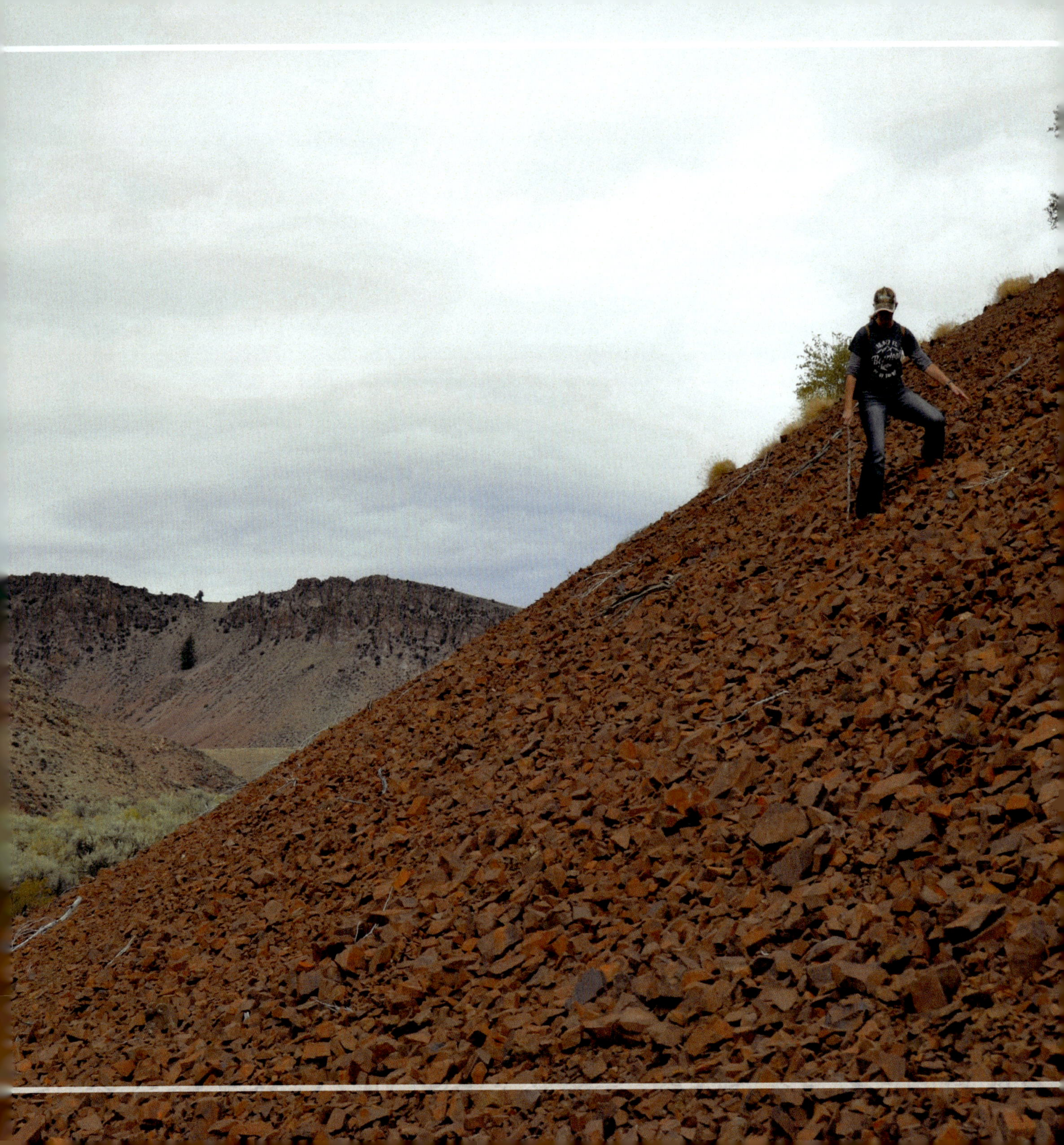

Scree

Scree is a large collection of small loose stones that form or cover a mountain slope. Even experienced hikers have a healthy fear of scree. As long as we are on a firm foundation, we can hope for a fighting chance to conquer the dangers in front of us, behind us, or even above us. But when the very ground we walk on cannot be trusted, the world seems somehow frighteningly unfair, unpredictable, and scary.

Christie: *How does a healthy young person, like my brother-in-law Josh, come down with a rare, terminal cancer? It didn't make sense. I wanted to know how this could happen so I could prevent it from happening to someone else. I started reading about chemicals, pesticides, and food preservatives. The more I read, the more worried I became—there are potential carcinogens everywhere! I found myself afraid to eat our food. Although learning to eat and live healthier should be encouraged, the fear I experienced was definitely not healthy.*

Experiencing severe personal tragedy casts a cloud over everything. We feel vulnerable, the world appears harsh, and God seems untrustworthy. Severe loss makes even the ground on which we walk feel undependable. While fearing scree is reasonable, we now fear asteroids, earthquakes, and alien invasions. Anxiety and distrust take on a life of their own. Though previously we drank readily from fresh mountain streams, we now imagine all kinds of hidden dangers lurking in the water.

We long for the previous feelings of safety and trust, but those feelings now seem distant, naïve, and unattainable. Our perception of the world seems forever changed. Yet perhaps this is not a permanent state. Perhaps we can regain our previous sense of trust. After being in a car accident, one feels vulnerable, anxious, and distrustful just getting behind the wheel again. Every oncoming car seems dangerous. But with time, we realize most drivers actually stay on their side of the road, and our trust is restored.

Similarly, as time passes after experiencing loss, our fear will lessen, and we will regain our ability to trust. Not all of life is scree. One cannot rush this return to normalcy, however, since regaining trust is a process. We need to be patient with ourselves. Eventually, the ground under our feet will feel solid again.

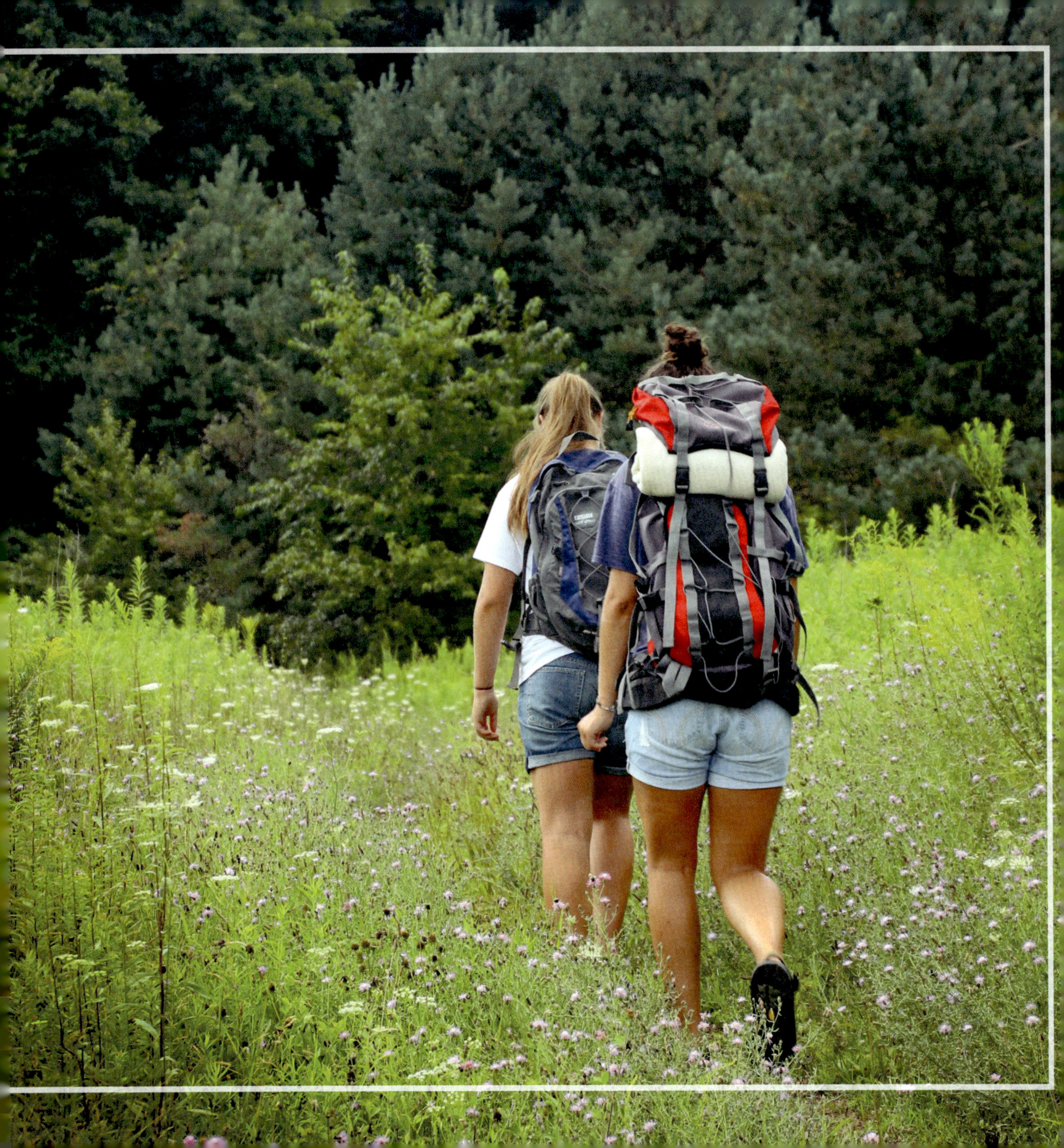

Travel Companions

Friends can be great companions along the grief journey. Often the friends who are most helpful are those who don't have all the answers. Platitudes like, "This is just God's will; she's in a better place now," or "God has a purpose in this," are rarely helpful. Grief is neither a question in search of an answer nor a problem requiring a solution. Grievers rarely require counsel on how to think properly about things but more commonly need compassion and empathy. Open ears and empathetic tears are more likely to be helpful than unsolicited advice and assurances of a heavenly home.

Friends who are most helpful will address the aching heart. Sometimes a friend just sitting in silence with us lightens our burden. It's been said that the duty of a griever's friend is to "show up and shut up." If words are spoken at all, they should usually be few and should address the heart: *I am here with you. I know you are in pain.* Author Megan Devine notes, "Some things in life cannot be fixed. They can only be carried." Grief needs to be carried, and burdens are lighter when shared.

While a friend's silent presence can sometimes be a gift, so can conversations of fond remembrance. Well-meaning friends often avoid mentioning the departed one's name out of fear of saying the wrong thing and hurting you more. For many persons, death is an awkward topic, and they are not sure what to say. As a result, they don't mention the missing person at all, which makes the one grieving feel like their loved one is not remembered. But sharing warm or even humorous memories about the one who is missed is often helpful in processing and sharing the weight of grief.

Some persons fear talking or thinking about death since it reminds them of their own mortality. They prefer to treat your grief like the chicken pox—keep it to yourself and get over it as soon as possible. Ironically, it may be Christian friends who have the most trouble with either intense or prolonged grief, both of which are usually defined *by the friend's* level of comfort. Whether verbalized or not, the subtle message is that if your faith were stronger, your grief would not be so severe—this is a harmful myth.

God also wants to accompany us on our journey with grief. While blaming God for our difficulties is tempting, He never promised us a life without struggle or pain. For God to make such a promise would be to deny the human state, the consequences of sin, and even the freedom to choose.

God does, however, *feel* with us in our suffering. We have a God who is full of compassion. Even more important, we have a God who has joined us in the human condition. When Jesus' friend Lazarus died and Jesus saw Lazarus' sisters grieving, "Jesus wept" (John 11:35). Upon receiving news of His cousin John the Baptist's death, Jesus withdrew from the crowds to a lonely place to grieve (Matthew 14:13).

Sometimes the reason we don't hear God's response to our anguished cries is that there are no words to answer our cries. Instead, He Himself is the answer; He is with us. Scripture reminds us that God will not fail or desert us, but *He will be with us* (Deuteronomy 31:8). God is our divine companion that is ever-present and ever-caring.

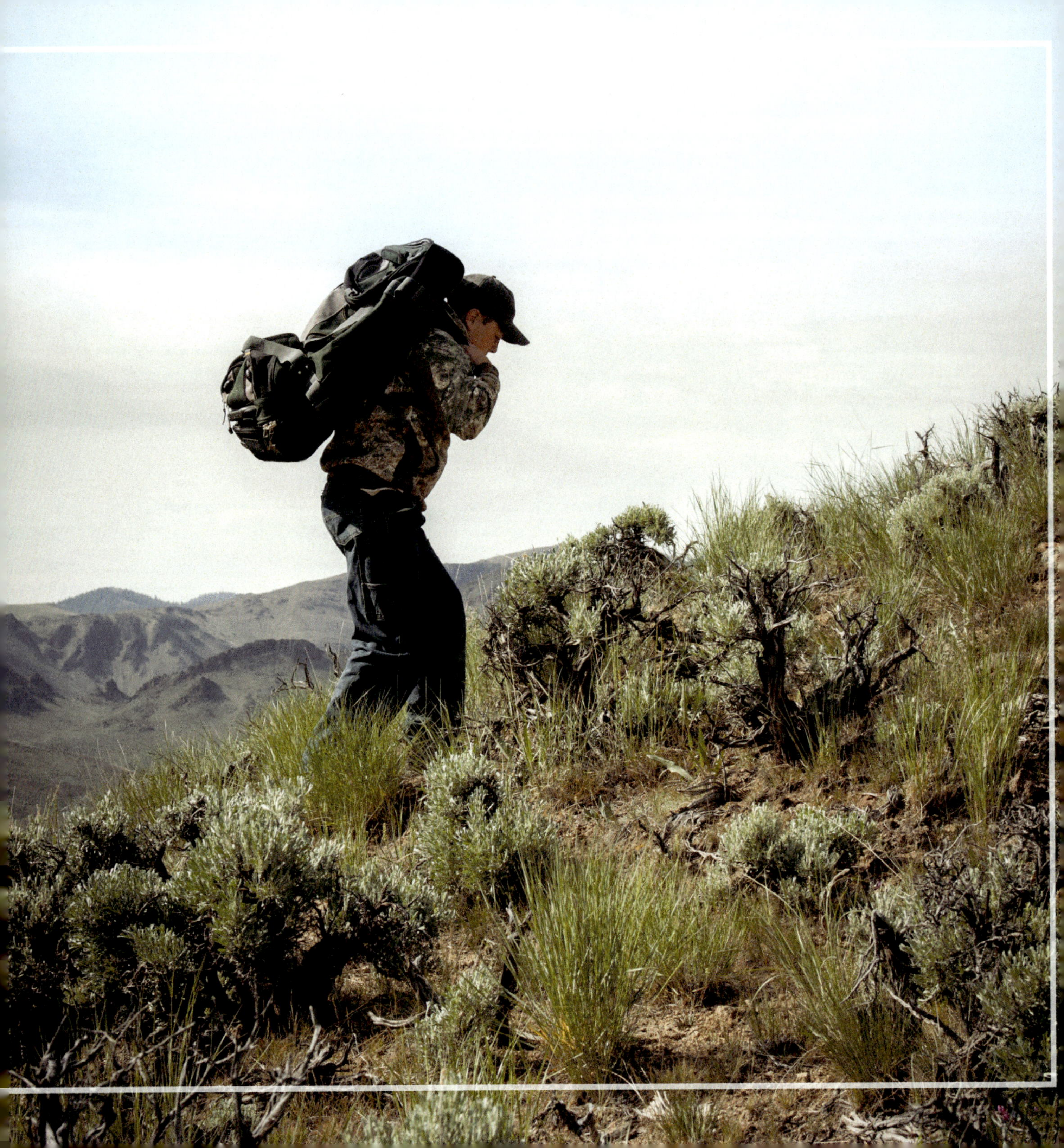

Unnecessary Burdens

Part of the difficulty in hiking Grief Mountain is that we drag along unnecessary burdens. Although these loads tire us out and slow us down, we tenaciously hang on to them. These burdens might include unforgiven hurt, unrealized expectations, or false guilt. We carry regret for feelings of anger or love that we never verbalized before it was too late. These burdens can sap our energy and deplete our joy and peace.

Christie: *My burden was that I had failed as a nurse. Nurses are supposed to make people better, yet I was unable to make Josh better. Of course, it was ridiculous to think I could cure him of a rare cancer that had stumped the doctors, but burdens don't always make sense. I would do a reality check and reluctantly put the burden down, but somehow without even thinking I would pick it up again. I had to lay it down multiple times before I was finally able to let it go.*

There are numerous reasons we are reluctant to give up needless burdens. Surrendering our heavy loads might mean giving up control or entitlement. It is difficult to surrender our anger toward a departed loved one who never apologized for deep hurts they caused us. It is also hard to yield our disappointment for unfulfilled hopes that were left dangling by their death.

I deserved such and such, and I'm entitled to be angry about not getting it. So by golly, I'm not about to give up these feelings! We cut off our noses to spite our faces, while stubbornly clinging to our heavy burdens.

In order to get rid of a burden, we first need to realize we have one. If we are single-mindedly focused on the hike, we might neglect to stop and inspect the contents of our surprisingly heavy pack. Unfortunately, becoming aware of the burden doesn't make it magically disappear. When we become mindful of our unnecessary load (e.g., anger, guilt, self-pity), we still need to be willing and able to lay it down.

As we let go of the load, its weight becomes clear as we feel new vitality in our steps. The freedom we can experience by letting go of our self-centered burdens cannot be anticipated; it is a God-thing, a spiritual and joyful surprise.

Yet giving up our burdens can also make us vulnerable by revealing previously hidden feelings or wounds. Surrendering control, unforgiveness, or entitlement can be scary, as our emotions lie bare and exposed. We wonder if we can trust God and our friends, as they carry our hearts in their hands, to be careful, compassionate, and caring. This type of unburdening requires emotional and spiritual courage, but it can make the hike much easier.

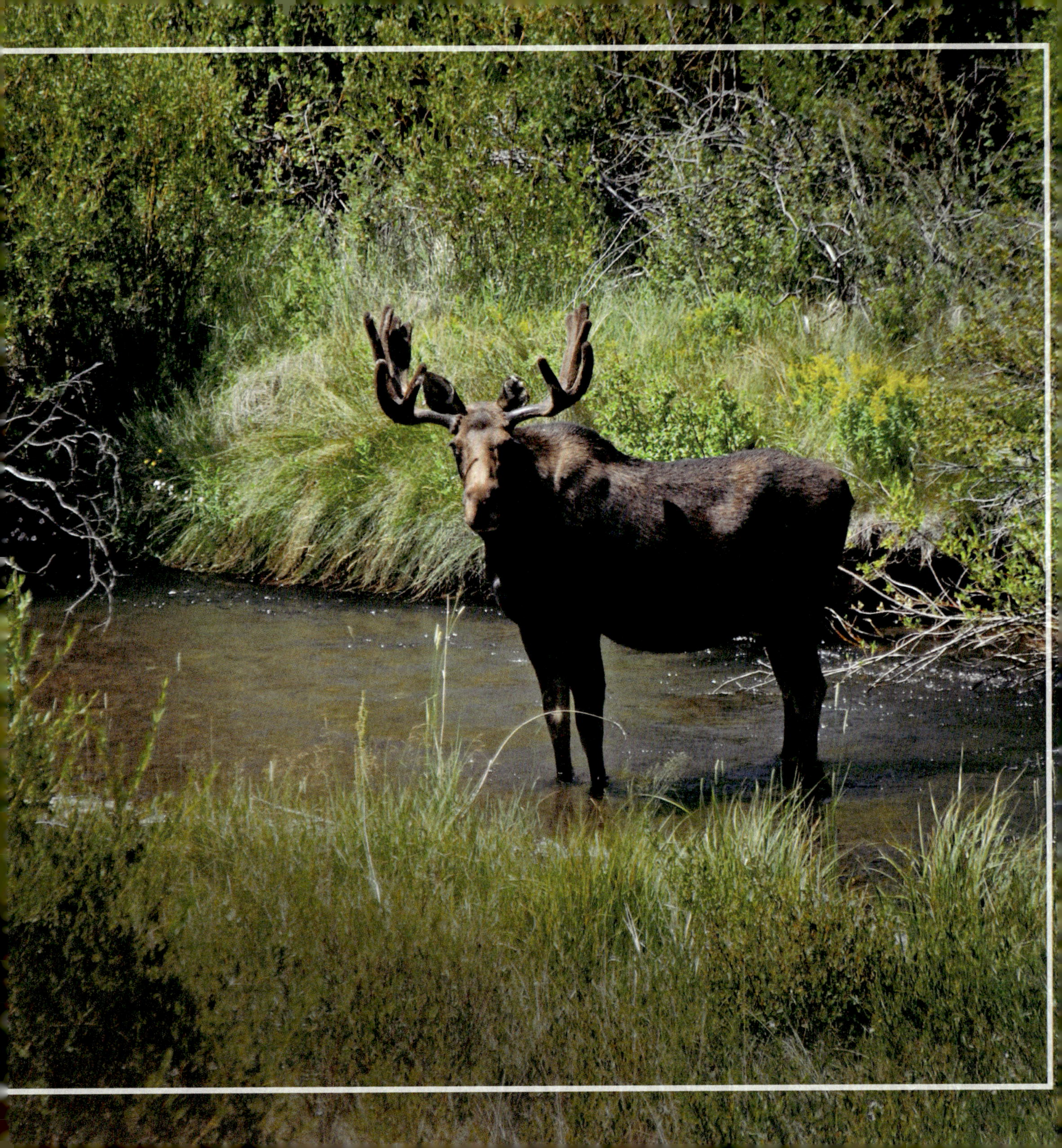

Uncertainties

It is always nice to know what to expect on a hike, but the truth of the matter is that there are a lot of inherent unknowns. The weather, the conditions of the trail, and who or what we will meet as we travel are all things we cannot know before departure. When the moose raises his head to look at us, is he just curious and granting us a great photo op, or is he about to put his head down and charge? We can try to anticipate animal behavior, personal injuries and accidents, but it all remains a very imprecise science.

When someone close to us dies, we find ourselves in a similar position, trying to navigate life while being forced to admit uncertainties. Like the hiker, we must continue to walk in spite of unknowns. Our uncertainties include hard questions that are difficult, if not impossible, to answer. *Why is there suffering? What happens after death? Will we face more tragedies? Is there any meaning to our existence?*

Philosophers and theologians have wrestled with life's uncertainties and hard questions for centuries. Interestingly, of all the creatures inhabiting our planet, we humans are the only ones who seem to ponder these mysteries. Rabbits have no curiosity about the existence of either foxes or carrots. Perhaps the fact that we wonder at all is a clue worth pursuing. Maybe the reason our lives contain wonder, doubt, surprise, and mystery is that we do not ultimately belong on earth as it is. The fact that suffering and death seem "wrong" to us may reveal something about *us*. Perhaps we were not created for death as the end but for life eternal.

Christian faith provides answers to some of humanity's most basic queries: *Where did I come from? Why am I here? And where am I going?* Yet even as persons of faith, we also must learn to live with mystery—not all our questions can be answered.

Our easy and spiritual-sounding explanations often crumble under the weight of devastating tragedy. Grief forces us to reexamine our spiritual assumptions that previously went unchallenged. Experiencing severe anguish moves our faith from the abstract to the concrete, from the head to the heart. Grief cannot be analyzed or clearly understood. We need to learn to live with unanswered questions.

Death forces us to reflect on these weighty, challenging inquiries that we are normally able to avoid considering. By forcing us to walk the uncertain trail of difficult questions where we can't see what lies ahead, grieving someone's death ironically helps us live life more fully.

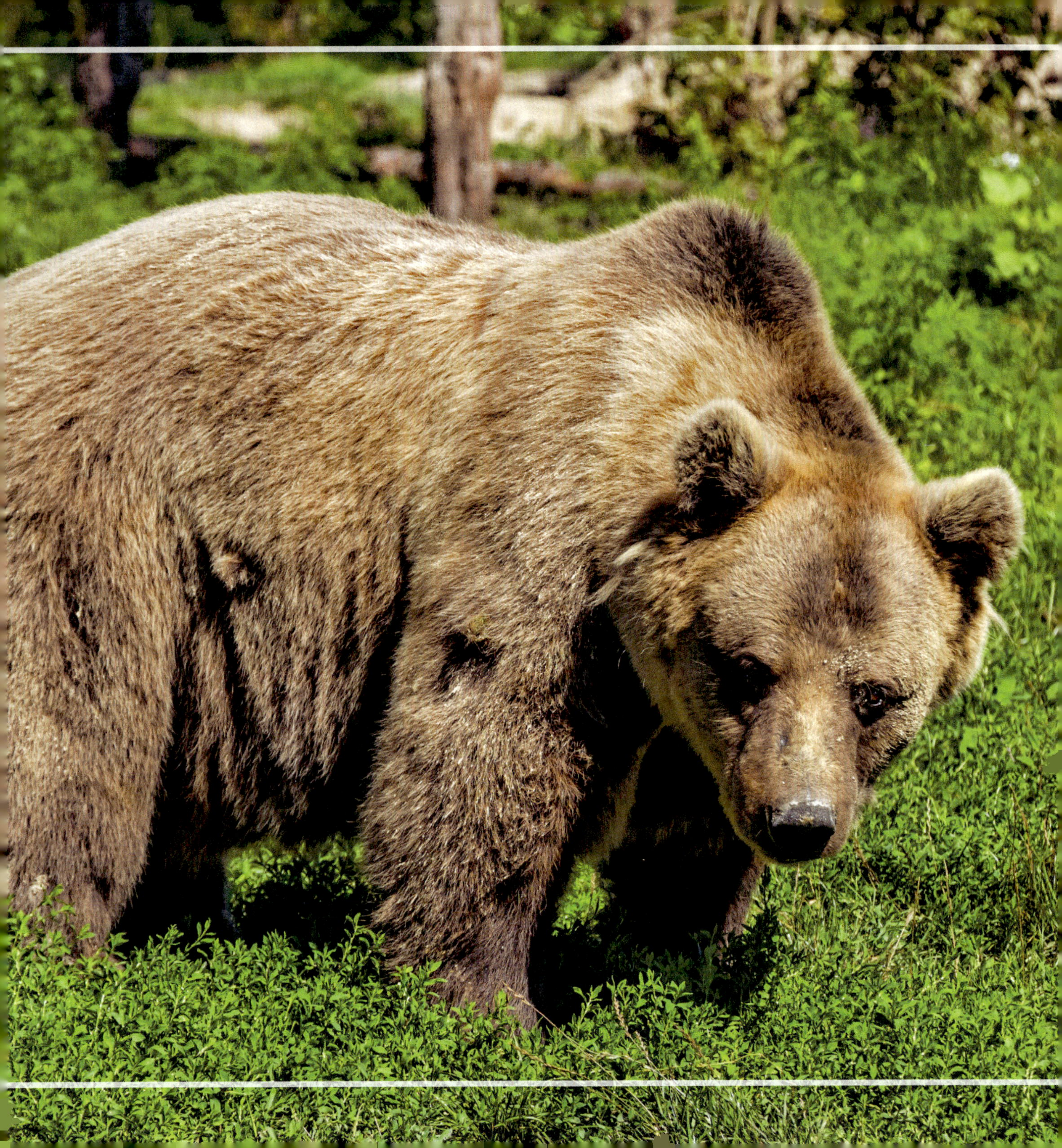

Don't Feed the Bears!

Some trails have signs placed by forest rangers. Although at times the instructions may make us feel like we're back in third grade, they are designed to keep us safe. A common sign on western mountain trails reads, "Don't Feed the Bears!" This placard serves two purposes. First, we are made aware bears might be in the area, so subconsciously we may pick up our pace. Secondly, we are receiving good advice to keep us protected. Feeding a bear may encourage him to follow us. When we run out of food for the bear, he may become irritable and suddenly less cute and cuddly.

Watching a bear in the wild can be interesting and even exciting. Typically, they go about their bear business and don't even seem to notice humans. Our naïve interest and desire to get a better photo, however, may not mesh well with the bear's desire to be left alone. The results could be tragic.

Sometimes we innocently approach negative memories that, like a bear, have the potential to harm us. These memories might include wounds of regret, emotional injury, or unresolved conflict. Replaying these memories only serves to irritate, not heal, old wounds. When every conversation, every activity, and everything we see or hear reminds us of our loved one's absence, they die a hundred deaths before it's time for lunch. This is unhealthy rumination, and allowing these negative thoughts to replay over and over in our minds is also "feeding the bears."

Surprisingly, at some level we may not really want our wounds healed. We have difficulty giving up our identity as a persecuted person who has a wound to prove it. We subconsciously pick at our wounds, preventing their healing.

On the other hand, if we are ready to let our wounds heal, recalling old memories can serve an important role as we progress through our mourning. Reexamining what happened and processing negative reflections is sometimes necessary for healing to occur. With the aid of a spiritual director, pastor, or mentor, we can sometimes revisit these painful scenes and become aware of God's presence and love in those difficult situations.

Talking to someone who is an empathetic listener is also helpful. Having been caringly heard and understood may help us better deal with negative thoughts and painful images. By avoiding feeding the negative memory bears, we can continue on our way more safely.

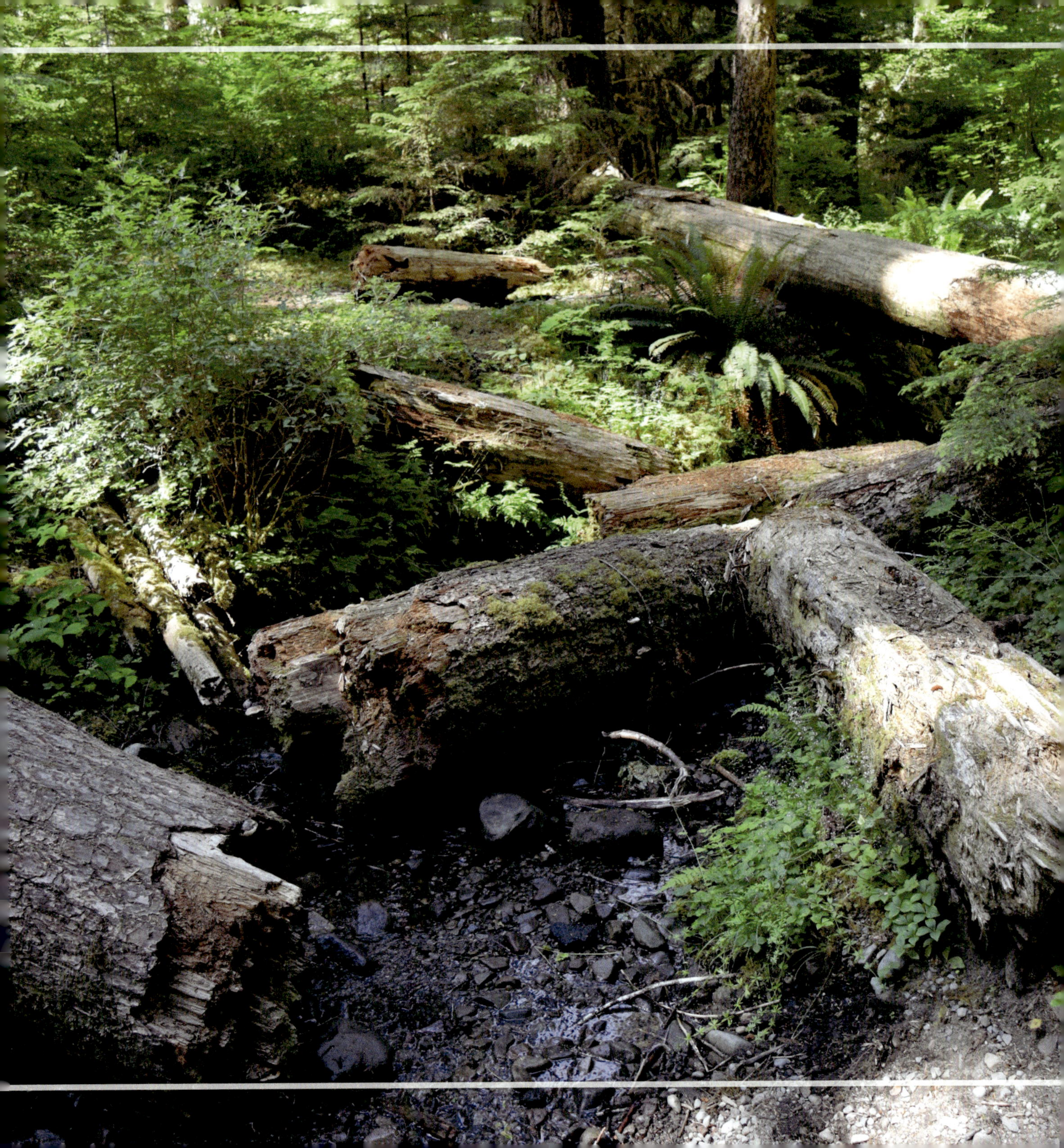

Obstacles

While some obstacles are surprises, others can be clearly seen even at a distance. As we approach logs on the trail, a boulder, or a high rock wall, a sense of dread wells up inside us. *How will we ever get past this?*

Some difficulties on our grief hike, such as birthdays, anniversaries, and holidays, are not surprises because we know they are coming. These days that were once happily anticipated are now awaited with anxiety, sadness, and even despair. Since we can no longer share these days with our loved one, we may prefer to avoid the celebrations altogether.

Planning ahead for these events can be helpful. Since annual traditions are often difficult after someone's death, we may be able to make some changes to decrease the pain of those days. For example, planning something special in memory of the loved one or including them by photo or story may soften the hurt of the day. Being with others who share our grief can also be beneficial.

Myron: *I remember the first Christmas after my dad died. Christmas had always been a very special time for Dad. He reveled in the family being together, the great food, and the fun games. To say his absence was strongly felt is too trivial a statement. Rather than pretend he wasn't sorely missed, we decided to share stories about Dad/Grandpa. For over an hour we told one story after another; some were humorous and some poignant. The stories were punctuated with tears and laughter, and we all healed a bit that night.*

Sometimes we just need to remind ourselves the day will pass and we will get through it. Some people find the *actual day* ends up not being as difficult as the anxiety leading up to the day. From a distance, a hiker dreads a huge boulder ahead, but she may sigh with relief when she arrives and finds handholds that allow her to scale it with minimal effort. The *first* birthday, anniversary, Christmas, Thanksgiving, etc., is usually the most difficult. Each subsequent year tends to be a little easier. The logs and boulders still lie on the path, but time seems to wear away at their impact.

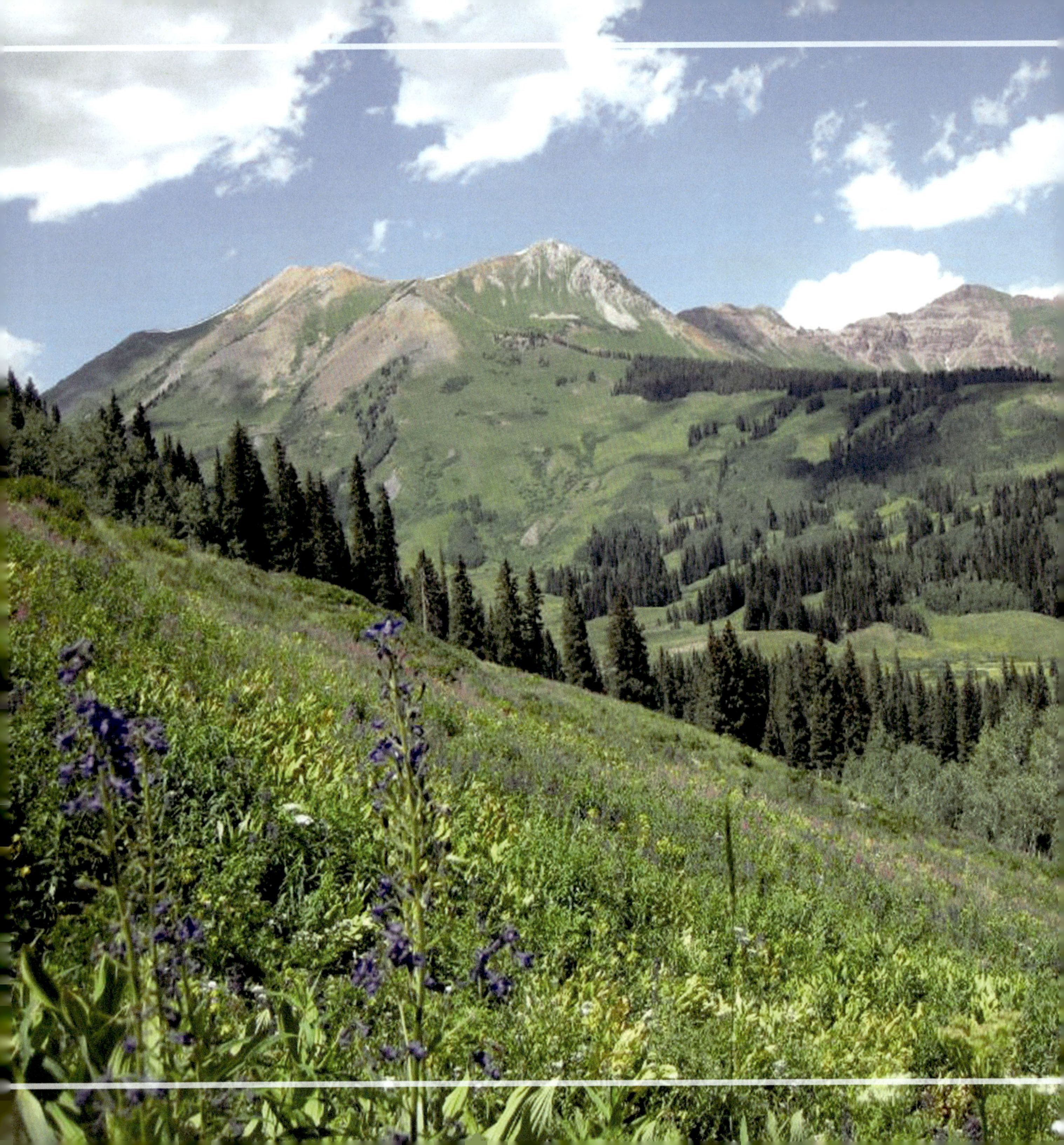

The View

Hiking can be monotonous. The routine drudgery of putting one foot in front of the other is about as exciting as watching ice melt. The hike, however, can be more than just walking a trail. A Yiddish proverb describes the problem of living a nearsighted life: "To a worm in a horseradish, the whole world is a horseradish."

If we can look beyond our "horseradish," our hike will have more to offer. If we lift our eyes off the trail, we notice a forest of lush trees, flowers of many colors, a croaking toad, a hopping rabbit, or a white-tailed deer bounding through the brush. Overhead are fluffy, white clouds accenting a blue sky that goes on forever. The beauty of nature can touch our hearts and give us a spiritual perspective for our sorrow. It is helpful to see beyond the trail and look beyond our grief.

The gentle beckon of music, art, friendship, and humor offer a remedy for the quandary of unending sadness and despair. They can serve to reopen our hearts to God's love and the love of others. Though our lives are forever changed, they can still be abundant, rich, and full of purpose.

The Old Testament prophet Jeremiah was so overwhelmed by grief that he wrote an entire book giving voice to his mourning. Nonetheless, in the midst of his sorrow, he was at times able to glimpse beyond his circumstances and declare: "[God's] compassions never fail. They are new every morning; great is your faithfulness" (Lamentations 3:22b-23).

Sometimes we are persistently unable to look past our severe grief. Although most grievers do not require professional help, this is not always the case. Warning signs that should prompt us to seek professional assistance from a therapist or physician include the following: 1) lack of a supportive community, family or friends; 2) persistent or recurring thoughts of hurting oneself or suicide; 3) maladaptive coping behaviors such as the use of drugs or alcohol; and 4) the persistent inability to reengage in the routine activities of daily life.

Although a severe tragedy has permeated every aspect of our being, the sun still rises each morning. And, as a song from the Sixties states, "the birds [do] go on singing." As we see that the earth continues to rotate on its axis, oblivious to our plight, we are gently nudged into the possibility that life for us may be able to continue. After all, God is still sustaining the universe, and there is still beauty and joy to be experienced. This wider perspective can slowly begin to engage our minds, heal our emotions, and refresh our spirits.

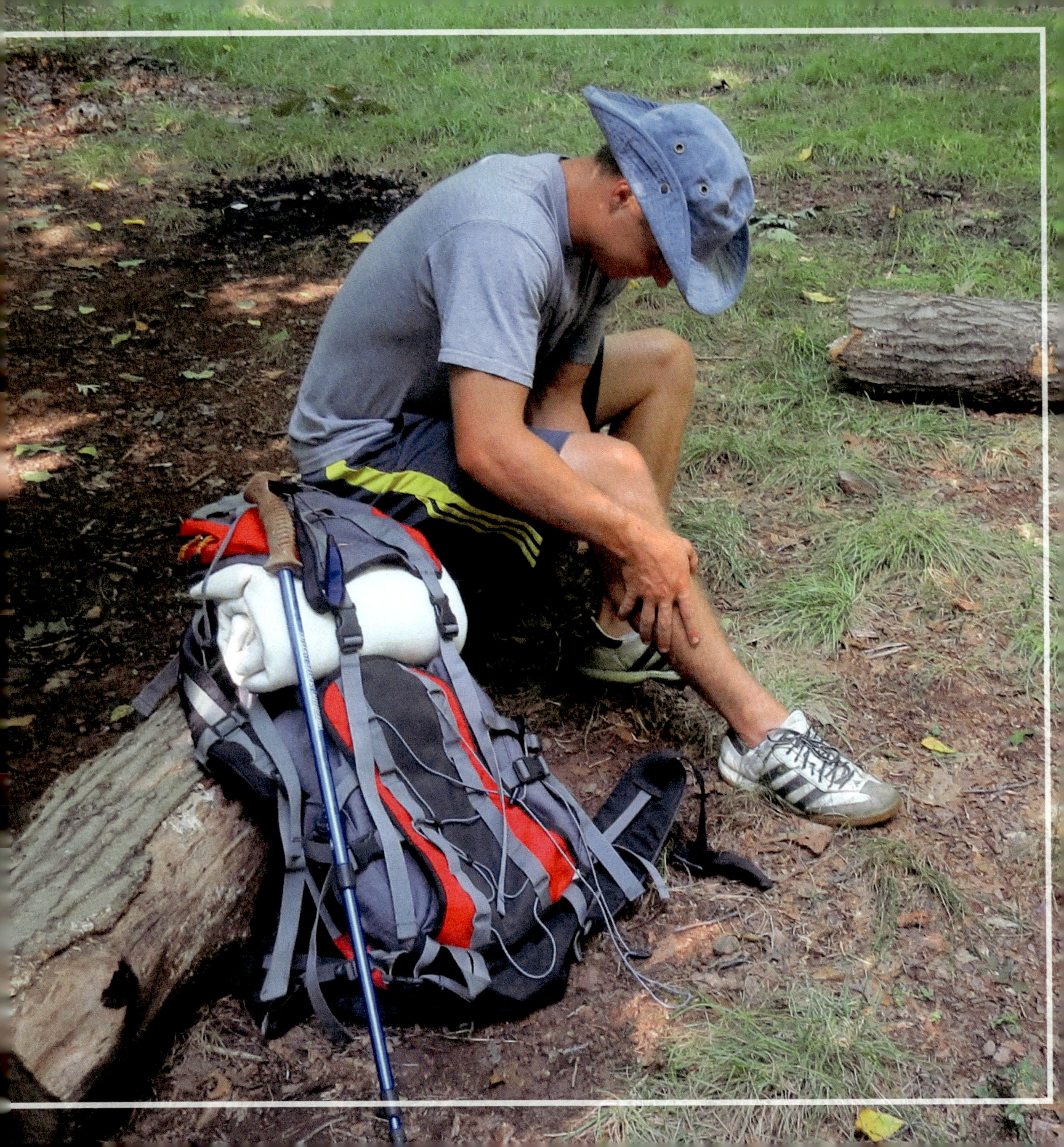

Muscle Cramps

Pain is our body's way of telling us something is wrong. There is nothing quite like a charley horse in the calf for catching our attention. Cramps can be caused by overuse of the muscles, dehydration, electrolyte deficiencies or injury. Lacking a voice box, the muscle's only way to communicate is by going into a spasm causing severe pain. *Can you hear me now?* The message is clear: *You need to stop this hike immediately. I have needs that are not being met. And until those needs are met, you are not going anywhere.*

Some of us are very goal-oriented. We started the grief journey in order to get to the end, and we would like to accomplish this objective as quickly as possible. Toward this end, we have been pushing ourselves pretty hard to finish this unwelcome hike. The process of grieving, however, has its own timetable and is very resistant to being rushed. To some degree, we must surrender to the grief process and let it take as long as necessary.

When a leg cramp interrupts our hike, our primary goal has been delayed, and we must stop to rest. Massaging and stretching the muscle can be helpful. Applying heat and drinking electrolyte-rich fluids can also be beneficial. When we're trying to push through our grief quickly and we hear the cry of pain, our unplanned stop is a call for internal self-assessment. *What's going on inside us to cause this pain? Grief is the painful process of adjusting to loss. What adjustment is causing our present pain?*

Many persons find journaling is a helpful tool for expressing the pain of our inner thoughts and feelings. A friend of John and Abigail Adams was killed in the Revolutionary War. Abigail sent a letter to her husband lamenting, "My bursting heart must find vent in my pen." Journaling allows us to vent our emotions and forces some introspection. In order to write down words to describe our feelings, we must first become aware of what they are. We can each write down the story of our own personal loss. *What do we miss most about them? What will we never forget? What are our varied feelings?*

When we are grieving, sadness is seldom our only emotion. We also feel guilt, bitterness, frustration, anxiety, dread, hopelessness, loneliness, or helplessness. Identifying these feelings through honest self-examination is an important step in processing them.

Journaling is not only helpful in evaluating our feelings but is also helpful in clarifying and handling our thoughts. Processing our thoughts involves considering where they came from, if they make sense, and how they are influencing our feelings and actions.

In addition to self-assessment, pain is often telling us to engage in self-care. Be kind, thoughtful, and gentle with yourself. Get a massage, go canoeing, or go to a concert or movie. Spend some unpressured time on a hobby you enjoy, or take time to be with a friend who is a good listener. Sit down under a shade tree and remember what you enjoyed about your departed loved one (this can be painful yet healing). Wait until the pain has subsided before moving on. Cramps are our body's messenger. We need to be sure the message is heard.

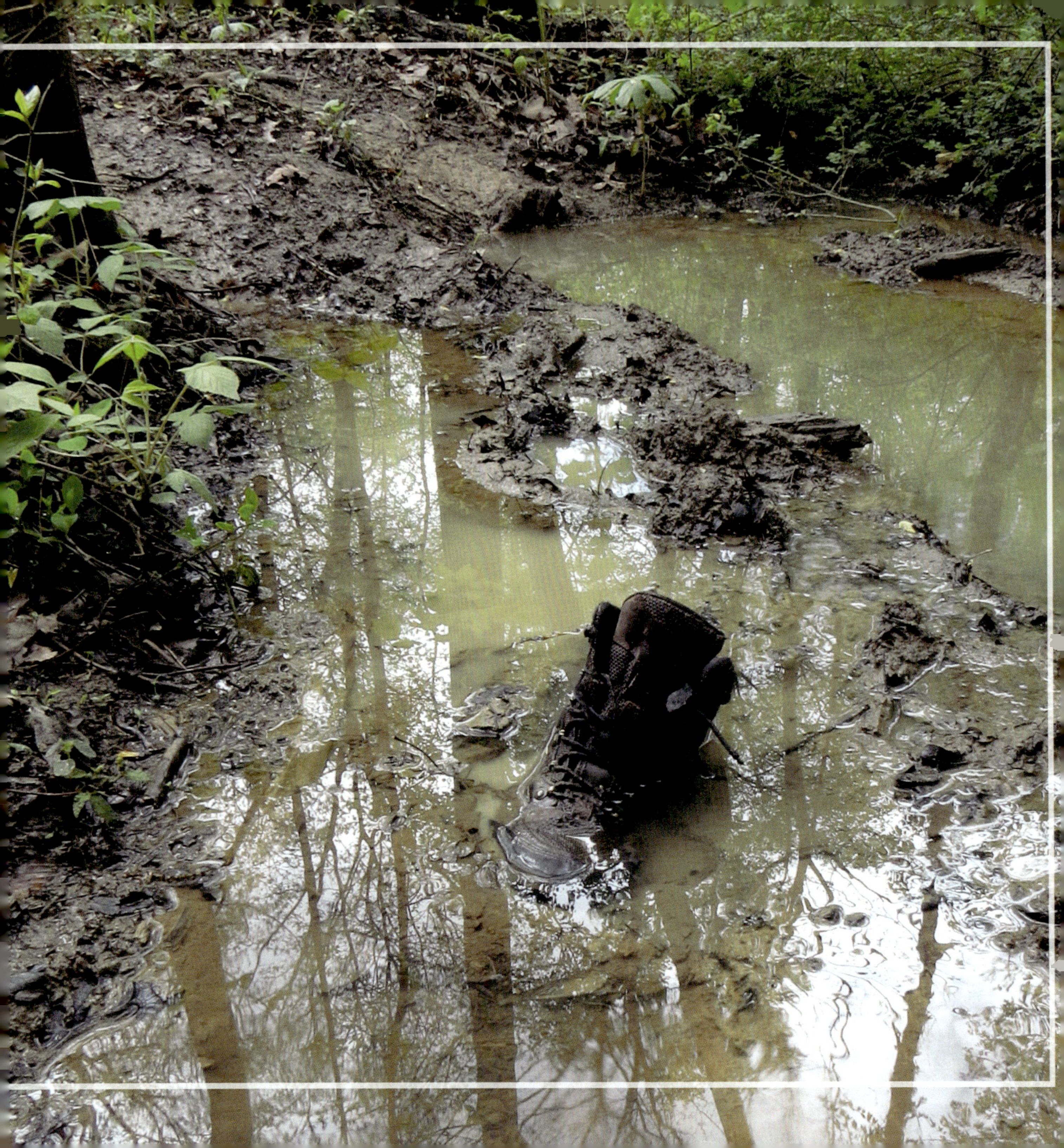

Stuck

Have you ever been stuck in some really nasty mud? I remember once being so stuck that I pulled my stockinged foot right out of my boot, which remained behind in the sludge. We can also get stuck in the grief process—usually due to fear, inertia, or guilt.

Fear: The Old Testament book of Exodus tells the story of former Hebrew slaves who endured a forty-year wilderness trek. This long journey led them from a life of bondage in Egypt to a life of freedom in Canaan (the Promised Land, "flowing with milk and honey"). Surprisingly, leaving the life of slavery they had known in Egypt was scary for them. As slaves they at least had steady work and food to eat. This wilderness trek was full of uncertainties. Although Canaan was supposed to be great, what if the milk went sour or the honey was full of dirt?

Similarly, when we feel totally torn out of the safety and certainty of our lives by a devastating disaster (like someone's death), the thought of moving ahead with life can be frightening. Even though staying where we are is terrible, we may fear an even worse disaster lies ahead of us. Yet one must admit that a life paralyzed by fear and stuck in the mud, is lacking in fullness.

Inertia: Changing their self-identity was also hard for the former Hebrew slaves. Being slaves and grumbling about the state of affairs doesn't seem like an enviable life, yet it had the comfort of familiarity. After four hundred years in Egypt, the Hebrews *viewed* themselves as slaves, and any change (even a positive one) was stressful. So, inertia set in. It was easier to stay where they were and not need to change.

In the same way, after a severe loss, we can develop an identity as an ill-fated griever, or even as a victim, and we may not want to change that self-image. As a victim, we receive special attention or sympathy that feels good. There is also a sense of security in that which is known, even when that which is known is being a lonely mourner or an unlucky victim.

Guilt: When we begin to make headway with the mourning process and start to feel like we will soon be ready to rejoin the human race, it is common to feel a sense of guilt. *How could I be getting over this loss? It's not right for me to be feeling better so soon. Didn't I really love them?* False guilt can act like an anchor tied around our neck and prevent progress in our grief journey. Our heads need to inform our hearts: *It's okay to feel better.*

Sometimes in our hearts, grief takes the place of our loved one. This makes moving on very difficult. We already had to give up our loved one, how could we be asked to give up our grief as well?

Getting stuck, in one way or another, during the grief process is a normal expectation. Staying stuck, however, is unnecessary and unhealthy. At some point, moving on is a decision of the will. We can choose to be unstuck, even if it means leaving an empty boot behind.

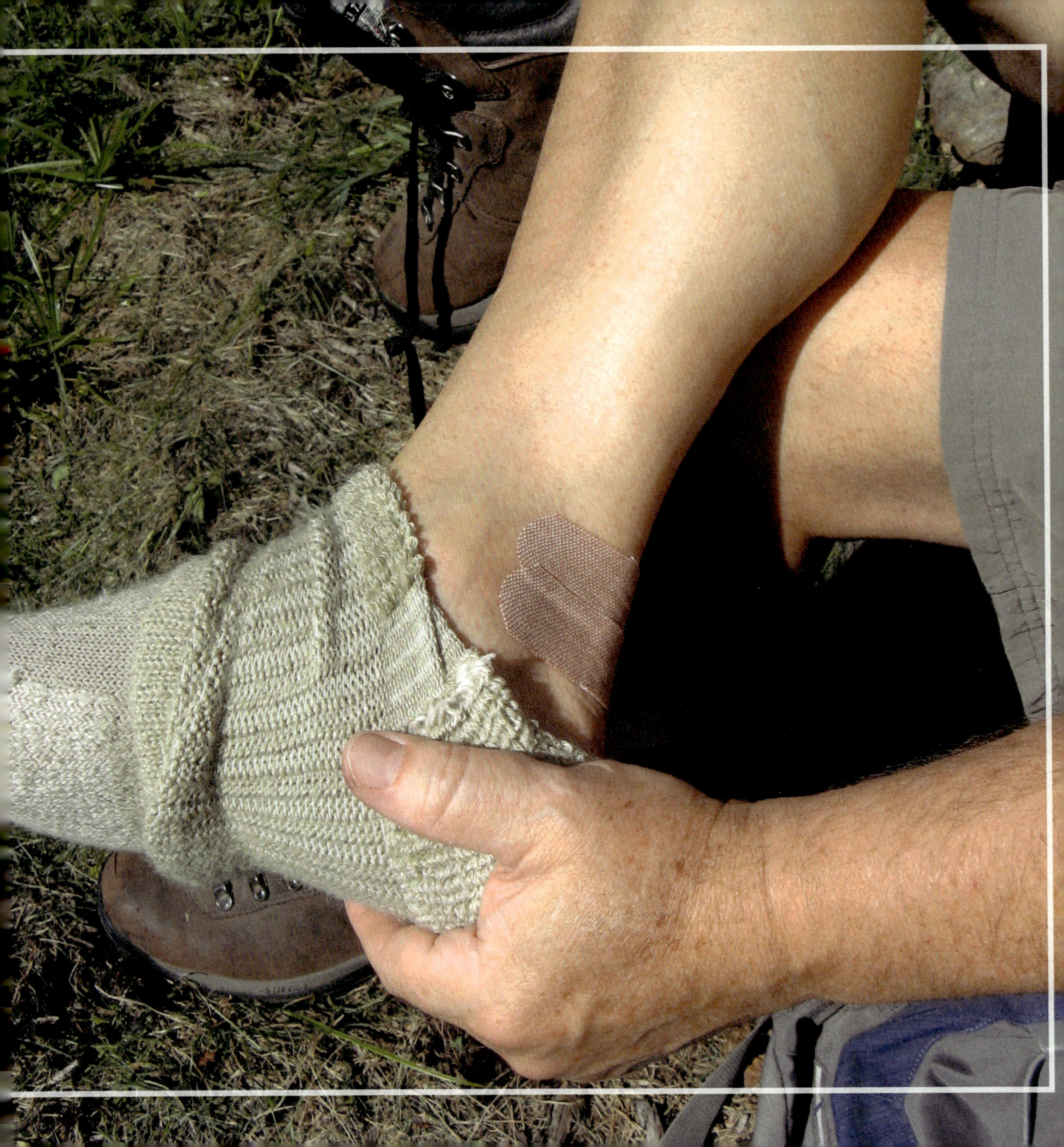

Blisters

No one has done much hiking without experiencing the painful malady of blisters. Each step is a reminder that we have a wound that is rubbed raw. While a Band-Aid or Dr. Scholl's cushion pad may help the pain from a blister, severe grief seems to be an injury without remedy. No medicine, surgery, or well-intentioned words can heal our gaping wounds.

Grief leaves no aspect of our being uninjured. Our bodies, minds, emotions and spirits are all under assault. Our bodies often experience overwhelming fatigue. Headaches and stomachaches are common. Our minds lose their ability to concentrate, and we find ourselves uncharacteristically forgetful. We wear our emotions on our sleeves, and these emotions are changing faster than a whirling pinwheel. Grief can also shake our spiritual framework. How could a good God let this happen? Why has God deserted us in our time of greatest need? Even our prayers seem to bounce off the ceiling.

Our wounds feel severe. Part of the problem with great loss, death or tragedy is that we did not choose it. While we know in our heads that these things are a normal part of life, our hearts are unprepared for their arrival. Pain is an uninvited, unwelcome, and unexpected intrusion into our imagined view of what our lives should be. Wounds create a vacuum within us, an emotional black hole that sucks up our hope, our joy, and our peace.

When someone close to us dies, we cannot *not* grieve. If we bang our thumb with a hammer, we will have pain. If someone dear to us dies, we will grieve. While we cannot choose if we will suffer grief or not, we can choose our response to that suffering.

For Christians, suffering and even death are not the end. Christ's resurrection provides a promise that there is life that follows death. This is our sure hope. It is because of this confidence that Paul said we do not grieve like those who have no hope (I Thessalonians 4:13-14). Notice that Paul does not say we do not grieve, but rather, he says we do not grieve *like* those without hope. We do still grieve.

Well-meaning Christians sometimes tell those in the throes of grief that they should not mourn so sorely. These words lack compassion and have the effect of poking at an open wound. Grieving can actually be an act of faith. Trusting God with our tattered lives, fragile feelings, and broken spirits is a vulnerable act of faith that honors God. Jesus said, "Come to me, all you who are weary and burdened, and I will give you rest" (Matthew 11:28).

As we hike, like all humanity, we will experience the painful blisters of life. But periodically, we catch glimpses of the summit that give us the strength and hope to persevere.

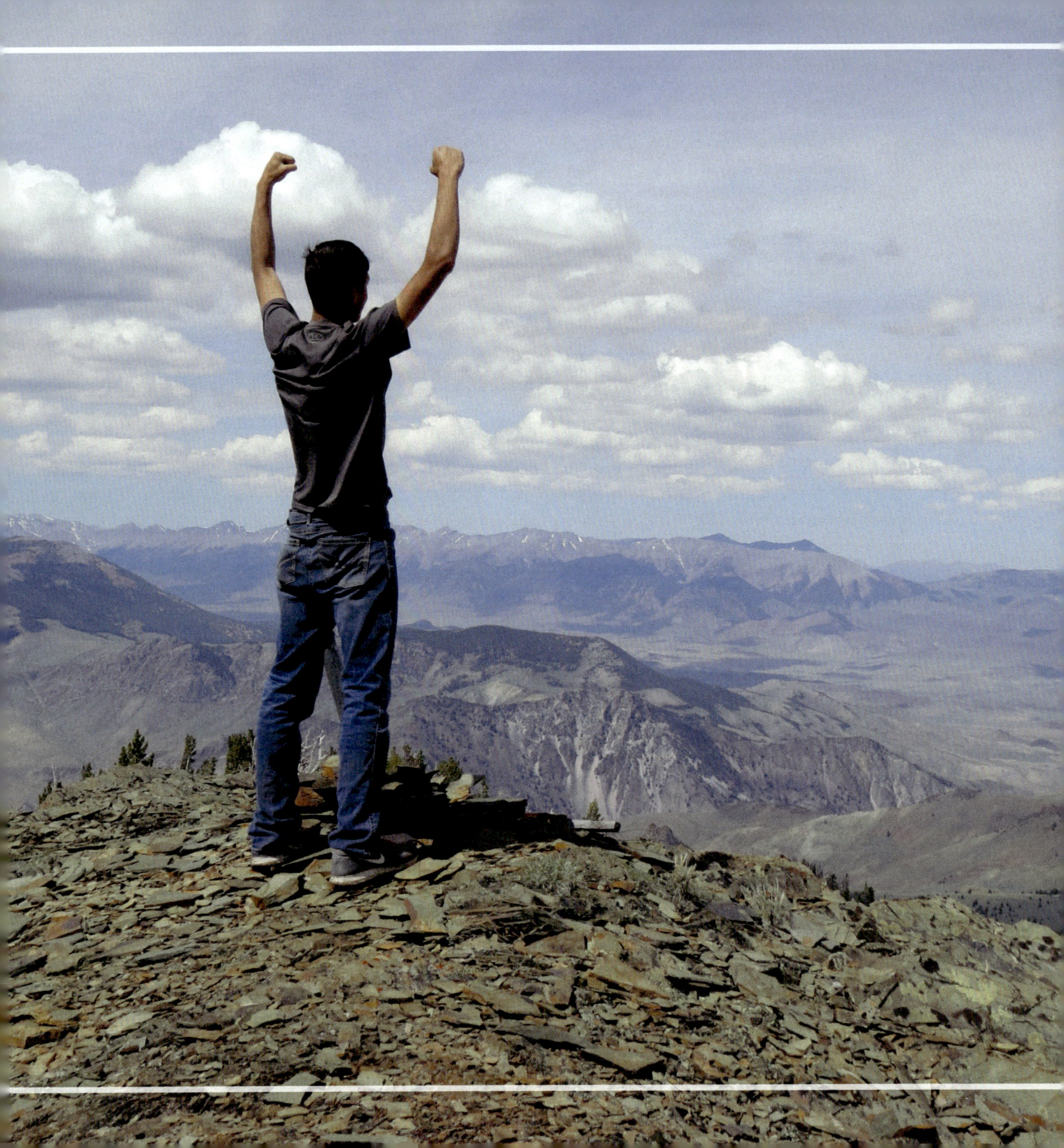

The Summit

At times it seemed we would never arrive. Some got here in a year. Others took two years or longer. There seemed to be always one more valley, one more hairpin turn, one more rise in the terrain that fell short of the pinnacle. But finally, we find ourselves at the top of Grief Mountain.

There is an almost euphoric feeling that makes us lightheaded. It was such a long and difficult hike! So many times we thought we couldn't continue. The slopes were just too steep, the backpacks too heavy, our provisions inadequate, and we simply were not in the physical condition needed to complete the hike. Yet here we are at last. The unattainable is now reality.

Previously, this summit *was* the goal. But the summit offers a new perspective. From here we can see the difficult path behind us, but we can also see the way that still lies before us. In one sense, we have "arrived." In another sense, our journey continues. Life continues after the grief summit. In grieving, like living, what is important lies in the process, not in getting to the end of it.

We previously thought we would conquer the trail. Now we see the trail has affected us, not vice versa. There is a sadness that on some level we will always carry with us. But we are also wiser, humbler, stronger, and more thankful than before. We have a greater appreciation for even the small joys and beauties in life.

It seems that with time our hearts have grown. Perhaps our hearts are larger because they carried so much sorrow for so long. Somehow because of this journey, our hearts now have the capacity to carry more love and more compassion than when we began.

Our perceptions on life and people have changed and developed. We are not the same persons who embarked on this journey long ago. This summit viewpoint gives us an opportunity for a more complete perspective on the significance and impact of our journey. By viewing our past while looking forward to the future, we are now better able to live in the present.

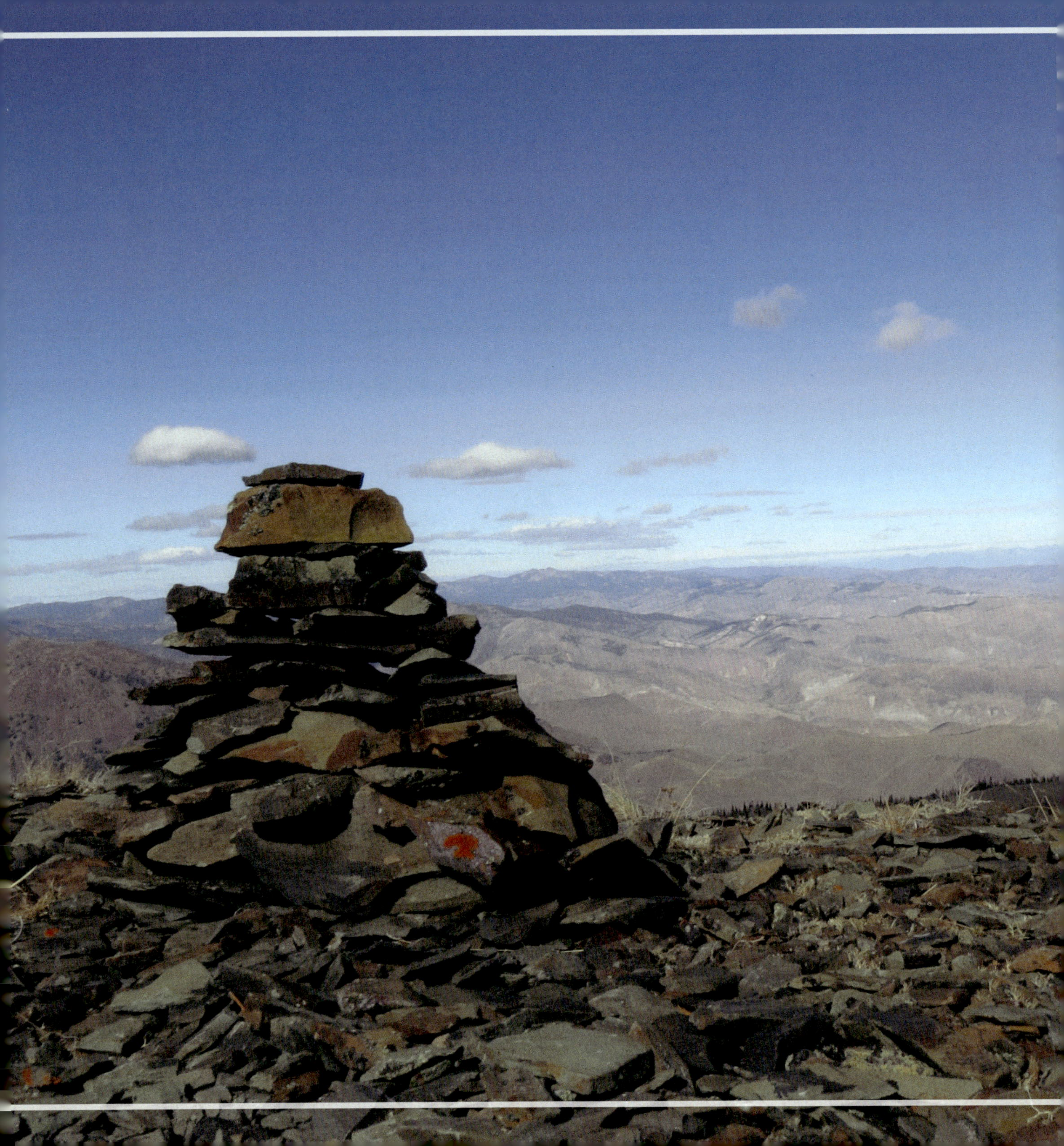

Monuments

A long and difficult hike that finally results in reaching the mountain peak is quite an accomplishment. Many hikers mark the completion of strenuous treks with some type of monument. Abstract feelings of accomplishment and success are somehow made more real, enhanced, and completed by using something visible and tangible to represent that feat. On some summits, conquering hikers will plant a flag. More commonly a stone will be added to a pile of stones formed by previously successful hikers. When one adds their own stone to the pile, it somehow augments the feeling of a successful achievement.

The use of monuments can also be helpful in the process of grieving. Using an image, an object or a ritual activity gives us something concrete to symbolize the abstract emotions we are experiencing. Going from the abstract to the concrete can have surprising benefits in handling loss. Monuments can be comforting and healing and can help us make progress in grieving.

We might make a collage with pictures from our loved one's life, or we could find a stone, a leaf, or a photo that somehow symbolizes our inner pain or processing of loss. We might write a poem, compose a song, or paint a picture. Releasing a balloon, saying a prayer, or lighting a candle in memory of our loved one are other tangible ways to honor the departed.

As we travel the highways, it is common to see a cross with flowers beside the road, sadly marking the spot where someone died in a car accident. Our cemeteries are full of tombstones—granite monuments memorializing the dead who are buried there. Funeral services are fashioned with ritual activities, concrete objects, and images. These are all avenues for using something more tangible to embody the abstract reality of grief. Making the vapor of grief more solid somehow helps us in the process of grieving and healing.

Myron: *I was with my father when he passed away at his home in Indiana. I will never forget the loving care with which the funeral director cared for my dad's body. He gently wrapped his body with the bed sheet, swaddled like a newborn. It had probably been eighty-three years since Dad was wrapped in that fashion; love was demonstrated on both occasions.*

My father was a pastor for most of his adult life. We placed his Bible in his hands in the coffin as a reminder of that life-long passion. Dad's favorite pastime was hunting deer. His casket was adorned with a figurine of a deer with a big set of antlers. At Dad's viewing, we told stories, we laughed, and we cried. Our mutual wounds bound us together as we shared memories, gratitude and profound loss. The Bible and the deer figurine reminded us of Dad's passions. Concrete reminders helped us remember who he was. And somehow, touching those memories made it easier to move on.

Love and grief are two sides of the same coin—having one means we will have the other; it is the currency of life. Monuments are a tangible way to express both our love and our grief.

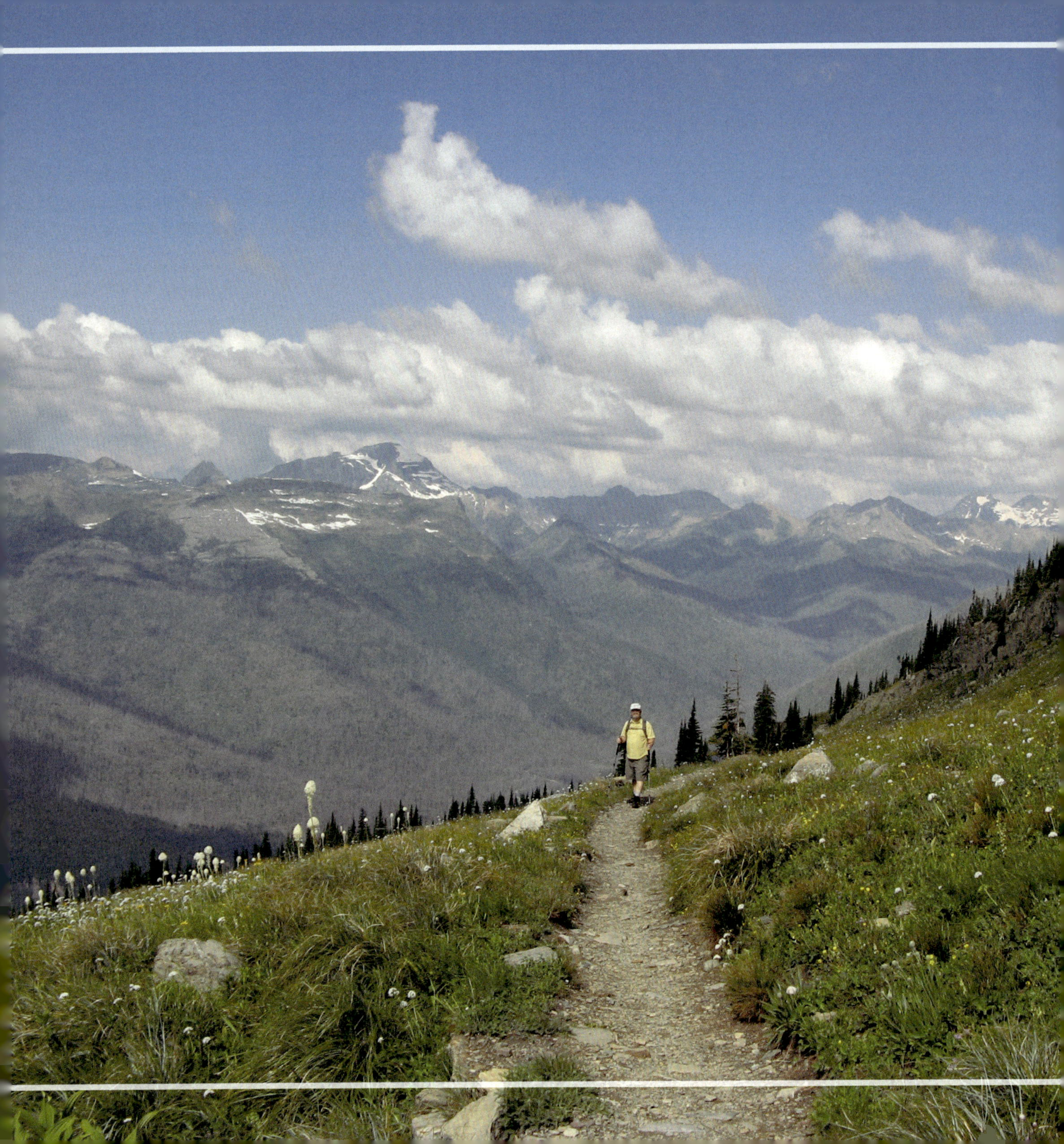

Trails End (or not?)

When we get to the end of a hike, does that mean our travelling is over? Although we are not on the same trail, we do continue to hike. And while we are no longer hoofing it on the grief trail, in some ways the old trail comes with us and becomes a part of who we are. The lessons we learned and the experiences we had are now imprinted on our lives. So in some ways, the old trail never really ends.

We hoped the process of enduring such great sorrow would somehow enable us to make sense of it all. But grief is like gravity—it is very real and we feel its force, yet it defies explanation. And it is so difficult to endure that which we are unable to explain. Nonetheless, we have endured, and we have grown.

When going through grief, many people talk about getting over it or "having closure." *Does complete closure really exist? And if complete closure does exist, do we need it or want it?* Wounds heal, but they leave scars. We rarely heal as though nothing had happened to us. If we hadn't loved our departed ones so much, our wounds wouldn't be so big. But that doesn't mean the loving wasn't worth the grief.

Often those around us push for us to "get over" our grief so that we can again experience joy. This line of thinking is often based on a fallacy. We don't need to be done with sorrow to experience joy. Author Anne Lamott describes grief: "It's like having a broken leg that never heals perfectly—that still hurts when the weather gets cold, but you learn to dance with the limp." It is encouraging to know we can still dance.

The art world offers a helpful parallel. Painters are so aware of the value of contrasting light and dark in pictures that they have a term, "chiaroscuro," to describe it. Similarly, joy and sorrow brushed simultaneously on the same canvas of our lives can produce a depth, a maturity, a beauty, and a realness that positively impacts those around us. We don't need to "get over" our grief. Instead, we learn to carry our grief *along* with joy, hope, and love as we continue our life journey. What happened to us internally during grief was so profound that it will take us the rest of our lives to plumb its depth. We hike on.

Author Addendum

Myron: On March 13, 2017, I received a phone call from my sister, Michele. Her son, my nephew, had been kidnapped in the Democratic Republic of Congo (DRC). Two weeks and an eternity later we got the devastating news that his body had been found in the Congolese jungle. The identity and motivation of the group that kidnapped and killed Michael remain unknown.

Michael Jesse Sharp, "MJ," was the only son of Michele and John, and the brother of Erin and Laura. Although he died at the age of thirty-four, he lived a fuller life than many ninety-year-olds. He had served in the Congo for five years, initially under MCC (Mennonite Central Committee) and then as the Coordinator of the UN Group of Experts on the Congo.

He spent his time in the Congo supporting victims of violence and negotiating with militia groups to try to find creative, peaceful ways to get militant soldiers to lay down their arms and return to their villages. He talked with militia leaders who had massacred women and children. He would listen to their stories to understand their perspectives and to look for some approach to motivate them to change their ways. His deep desire was to find nonviolent solutions to decrease the senseless violence and deaths in the Congo.

Speaking about the Congo, MJ once commented that, "places of intense conflict are also places where creative solutions are born and put to the test. Honestly, there's nowhere I'd rather be right now." Writer John A. Shedd coined a statement that describes MJ: "A ship is safe in the harbor, but ships were not meant to stay in the harbor." MJ was not meant to stay in the harbor, and he didn't. MJ engaged life and challenges head on. He was very bright, humorous, and an amazing storyteller. This past Christmas our family sat around in a circle listening to MJ tell stories of his life in the Congo for over an hour. It is hard to believe he is now gone.

In the weeks following his death, I went to work, I mowed the lawn, I bought groceries, and I went to church on Sundays. On the surface my life continued as before. But the invisible, inescapable reality, as ever-present as the air I breathed, was that M.J. was gone. He was swiftly, brutally, unbelievably, and irrevocably gone.

Writing a book on grieving failed to immunize me adequately against the heavy cloud of sadness and deep pain that enveloped me with his cruel death. The impact of my grief was cushioned somewhat by many caring emails, texts, Facebook notes, cards, prayers, kind words and tears.

Although I knew there are rarely satisfying answers to the "why" questions when faced with tragedy, it didn't keep me from asking them with great passion and anguish. *God, why did you let this happen? Weren't you watching this calamity unfold? This was so wrong, so unjust—don't you care?*

During the two weeks MJ was missing, thousands of people were fervently praying, seemingly to no avail. *How can I ever pray again? Does prayer really matter?* I yelled at God, and then I cried.

I was reminded of John 6 when Jesus shared a "hard teaching" with his followers—it was hard for them to understand and hard for them to accept. As a result, the gospel writer says that many of Jesus' followers "turned back and no longer followed him" (6:65-66). Jesus then asked the Twelve if they too would leave. Peter, ever impulsive and never at a loss for words, spoke up: "Lord, to whom shall we go? You have the words of eternal life. We believe and know that you are the Holy One of God" (6:67-69).

Ultimately, this is my response. I know God is good—He is loving and just. This truth does not unravel when I can't understand God's actions or inactions. Because of the premium God places on love, He gives humans the ability to choose to love Him or not. True love cannot be pre-programmed or coerced. As a result of this ability to choose, our world is broken, and we will experience suffering, pain and death. But one day all this will be made right, and all things will be redeemed. In the meantime, we can rest in the assurance that *nothing* can separate us from God's love.

I know that even though I cannot understand how God could let this happen, He is not distant from my suffering. I know He remains with me, and in me, and when I feel ready to collapse under the weight of grief, "underneath [me] are the everlasting arms" (Deuteronomy 33:27). The tears I shed are mingled with the tears of my triune God.

As Christians, we may mourn our losses deeply, but we know death is not the end. MJ's memorial service was on the Saturday between Good Friday and Easter. The promise of Easter was poignantly clear. Death has been defeated, and therein lies our sure hope!

Having this tragic event occur while writing this book on grief caused me to pause. I reread the text of the book, making some changes based on my present experience. The changes tended to be adding more "heart" and less "head." Christie was very patient as I dragged my feet on finishing the modifications.

Even though all of us have our own unique journeys, we are nonetheless fellow-pilgrims. Each of our journeys of joy and hope has been or will be punctuated by periods of grief. We hope that what we have shared may in some way be helpful to you when you struggle with your own sorrows.

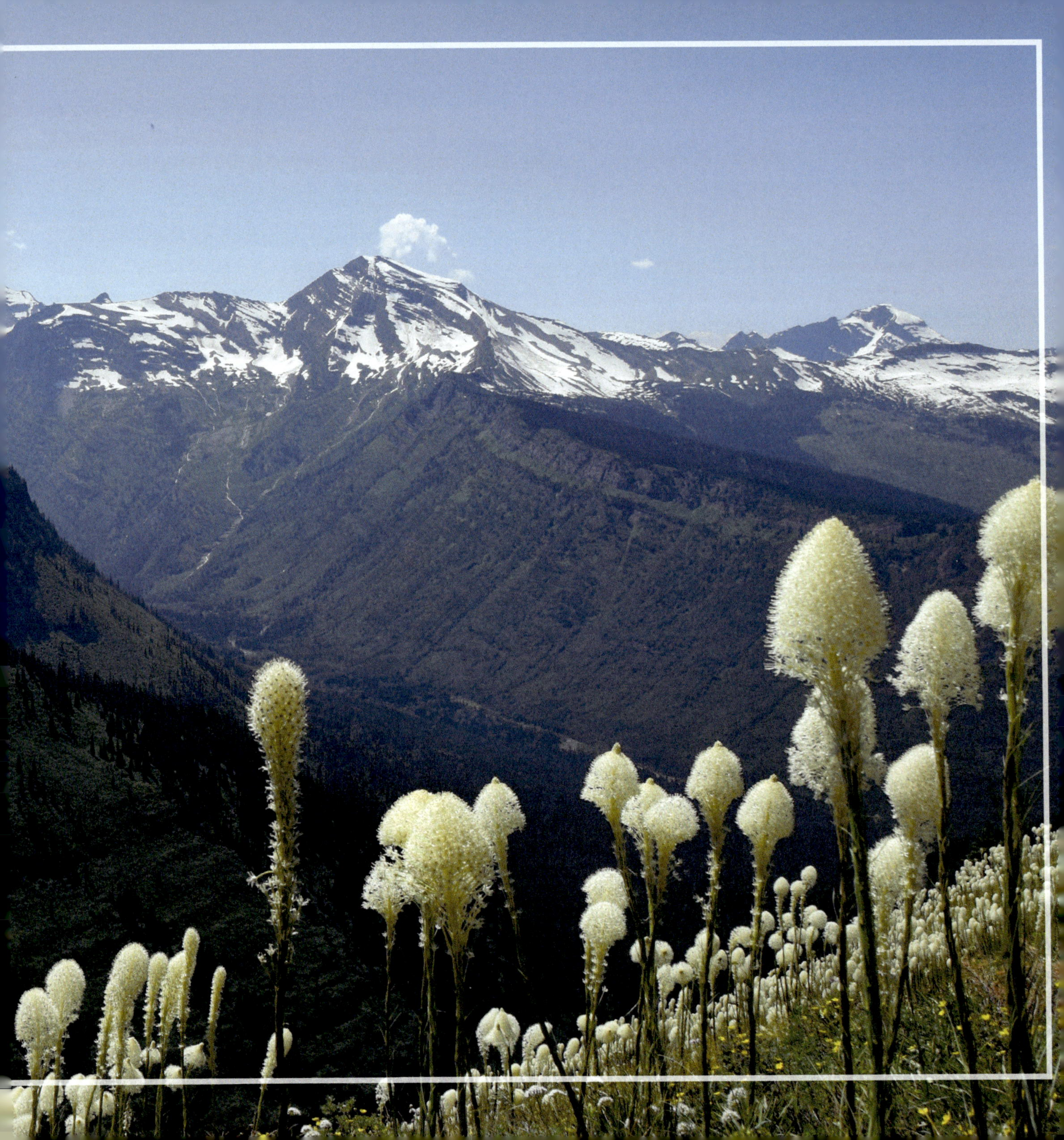

Vending Machine God

By Christie Ollar

Sometimes I think that if I pray
and keep my life pristine,
God should give me what I ask
like a vending machine.

I put my money in the slot—
good deeds and prayer-worn knees.
I ask God for the thing I want
and push the coded keys.

I wait for it to come my way,
Sometimes it moves so slow.
But surely it will one day come
and drop to me below.

I reach inside and pick it up
then thank God for His care,
for giving me just what I need
since I'm His child and heir.

I only ask for things I need,
like cancers to be gone,
for pain and hurt to disappear
and rid the world of wrong.

Then everything will be set right,
I would no longer fear.
As long as I just do my part,
my answers will be here.

But is this what I really want,
a God I can control?
Could I really love this God,
with heart, and mind, and soul?

And maybe I'd mess up His plans,
the ones I cannot see.
His plans with other lives involved,
not just those close to me.

I guess I want a sovereign God
with His *own* plans for me—
the One who walked on dusty roads,
yet stood upon the sea.

He gives me what I truly need
at each and every hour.
This God is strong; His name alone
can make the demons cower.

In Him is life, and to His own
He gives His very breath.
And due to His great love for me,
my God has conquered death.

If I would only trust His Word
that tells me not to fear,
I'd have more peace along the way
since He is always near.

In Him alone I have sure hope,
a hope that never fails.
It's Jesus Christ, my Living God,
whose love for me prevails.

About the Authors

Myron Miller is a physician in a rural family practice clinic in Pennsylvania. He enjoys reading, hiking scenic mountain trails, and writing. He is married and has four married daughters and six grandchildren. Myron is also the author of *Think on These Things,* a devotional book.

Christie Ollar worked as a nurse at the same family practice clinic as Myron. She and her family recently moved to Challis, Idaho where she continues to work as a nurse. Christie is married and has three sons. When not working at the clinic you might find her at one of her son's baseball games, reading, and/or eating chocolate.

Made in the USA
Lexington, KY
07 December 2017